MILTON

Samson Agonistes

MILTON

Samson Agonistes

EDITED BY

F. T. PRINCE

OXFORD UNIVERSITY PRESS

OXFORD
UNIVERSITY PRESS

Great Clarendon Street, Oxford OX2 6DP

Oxford University Press is a department of the University of Oxford.
It furthers the University's objective of excellence in research, scholarship,
and education by publishing worldwide in

Oxford New York

Auckland Bangkok Buenos Aires Cape Town Chennai
Dar es Salaam Delhi Hong Kong Istanbul Karachi Kolkata
Kuala Lumpur Madrid Melbourne Mexico City Mumbai
Nairobi São Paulo Shanghai Taipei Tokyo Toronto

Oxford is a registered trade mark of Oxford University Press
in the UK and in certain other countries

© F. T. Prince 1957

The moral rights of the author have been asserted

Database rights Oxford University Press (maker)

First published 1957

20 19 18

ISBN 0 19 831910 X

Printed Hong Kong

CONTENTS

INTRODUCTION

'PARADISE REGAIN'D ... To which is added *Samson Agonistes*' was published, Milton's last volume of verse, in 1671. The minor epic and the tragedy had probably occupied Milton since he had completed *Paradise Lost*, which appeared in 1667. But for the first conception of *Samson Agonistes* we must look back nearly thirty years, to a manuscript note of Milton's youth.

Milton was thirty when he set out for Italy in 1638, intending by this tour to complete his education as a poet. Probably not long after his return to England in 1639, he made a list of themes for dramatic poems, noting in some cases the treatment he proposed. There are subjects from the Old and New Testaments, from ancient British and Anglo-Saxon and medieval English history.[1] The story of Samson suggests a group of plays, among which his triumphant death occurs under the title of *Dagonalia*. Milton's first thought even at that time was for the primal and fundamental drama of the Fall which he proposed to call *Adam Unparadiz'd*; it is the most fully worked out of these synopses. But when, more than twenty years later, he came to write a tragic drama, he had not only disposed of that 'great argument' in his epic: he could see in the life of the Hebrew champion, as he could interpret it, a fitting emblem of his own active life during the interval, his 'race of glory' and 'his race of shame'.

Milton was not ready for such a subject, and could not have done it justice, until his last years. Few of the other

[1] The notes are preserved in a manuscript at Trinity College, Cambridge. See the Facsimile Edition by W. A. Wright, Cambridge, 1899, and vol. xviii of the Columbia Edition.

subjects he had fancied could have been developed, like this, into 'a survey at a single glance of the hazards and changes of human life'.[1] Perhaps only the proposed *Dagonalia* could have been used at last as Milton uses it, to look back upon his life of action and to affirm its final meaning. Human life, the destiny of mankind, is of course the theme of all tragic drama; but Milton's fable was chosen to refer also to his own arduous career.

That career was determined by Milton's conception of great poetry and of the true poet's task. In this there was a meeting of various traditions, all bound together by this poet's own intense convictions. There was the Greek and Roman idea, revived in Renaissance criticism, of the poet as not only an artist, a 'maker', but a sage or a seer; this was supported by the evidence of the Old Testament, in which the succession of Hebrew prophets spoke as poets to the people of Israel, exhorting them by means of visions and songs. To this classical and Biblical tradition Milton added the Puritan fervour of his own time and nation, convinced that the Holy Spirit must move, and even be seen and felt to move, in every true believer.

Milton had dedicated himself to poetry in his youth; as he prepared himself, by thought and study, England began to be stirred into spiritual debate, and he soon saw clearly, as he thought, the part a true poet must assume. Although he might not 'do great things', he could 'teach how they may be done', or 'describe them with a suitable majesty when they have been done'.[2] He gave as his motive for returning

[1] This phrase occurs in a Latin note on Tertullian in Milton's Commonplace Book: '. . . what in the whole of philosophy is more impressive, purer, or more uplifting than a noble tragedy, what more helpful to a survey at a single glance of the hazards and changes of human life?' See the Columbia Edition of the *Works*, vol. xviii, pp. 206–7.

[2] *Defensio Secunda* (1654).

to England from Italy in 1639 the beginnings of civil strife at home: great issues were to be decided, great religious and political questions would be opened; and at such a time no man of Milton's temper, and with his conception of his calling, would wish to remain abroad.[1]

The meeting of the Long Parliament in 1640 was the signal for intense public discussion of reforms in Church and State. Milton then put forward his own views in the first series of his prose tracts, those dealing with Church organization. These were soon followed by his plea for greater freedom in divorce, which met with much hostility. Much in all Milton's controversial writings is bitterly expressed, perhaps as bitterly felt; but Milton always kept in mind his conception of himself as the celebrant of great deeds, and a man akin to the Hebrew prophets, with a divine (though perhaps unwelcome) message to the English people: for, 'when God commands to take the trumpet and blow a dolorous or a jarring blast, it lies not in man's will what he shall say or what he shall conceal'.[2]

As the Civil War ran its course, and the various parties revealed their aims more clearly, Milton found himself less and less in agreement with any of them. The best known of his prose works, the *Areopagitica* (1644), was written to protest publicly against the Parliament's desire to suppress freedom of expression: a scornful sonnet of the same period gives the full measure of his disapproval.[3] It was not long before Milton saw, and may have rejoiced to see, that he was 'a sect to himself'. But this intellectual independence did not prevent him from accepting a post in Cromwell's

---

[1] *Defensio Secunda* (1654).

[2] *The Reason of Church-Government* (1641) The Second Book (*Complete Prose Works of John Milton*, Yale, 1953, vol. i, p. 803).

[3] *On the New Forcers of Conscience under the Long Parliament.*

Government. Given the task of defending the execution of Charles I, he could do so with both confidence and a clear conscience. Milton now wrote in Latin, the international language of his time, for he addressed himself to Europe, horrified by revolutionary violence in England. The controversy brought him European fame, and the sense of having achieved much in the national cause.[1] Ignored as a prophet, he was welcomed as a champion.

It was at this time, in the course of completing his Second Defence of the English people, that Milton lost his sight; and it was probably also at about this time that he began to fear that the Puritan cause would ultimately be defeated. Neither the nation as a whole, reluctant to press on to 'a reform of reformation', nor the behaviour of successive Parliaments, nor the policies of the Lord Protector, came up to his high expectations. Total blindness compelled him at length to relinquish his post as Latin Secretary. After Cromwell's death in 1658, it became obvious that Charles II would be recalled from exile. In 1660 the Commonwealth was abjured, and many of its chief figures pursued and punished. Milton, now a private citizen, remained unmolested, though in reduced circumstances, 'on evil dayes though fall'n, and evil tongues'. He completed the great epic which he had had to postpone for so long; and having completed it, became an object of respect and admiring pilgrimage. Yet Milton, as a poet, was above all a moral being, living the life of the mind and the spirit; and we cannot doubt that to him the England of Charles II was an abomination, as the return of the dog to its vomit. The repudiation by the English people of their priceless chance to achieve national regeneration was for him a tragedy dark enough to over-shadow all his later life.

[1] See the Sonnet *To Mr.* Cyriack Skinner *upon his Blindness.*

Those last fifteen years of retirement and poetic creation must be imagined also in the light of his private life. The history of his first marriage at least cannot be omitted in any account of his poetic development, and certainly not in connexion with *Samson Agonistes*. Yet after all we do not know a great deal about it. He married Mary Powell in 1642, after an acquaintance and courtship which seem to have been brief. After some weeks of married life, Mrs. Milton returned to her parents' home in Oxfordshire, where she remained until 1645. She then returned to her husband (it is said that she sought a reconciliation), and lived with him until her death in 1652, bearing him four children. Milton married again in 1656, but his wife died in childbed a year later. His third wife, whom he married in 1663, survived him.

It was in the period which followed Mary Powell's failure, or refusal, to return to her husband, that Milton wrote the tracts which make a plea for divorce on the grounds of what is now called 'incompatibility of temperament'. From his account of such a married state, we may conjecture that he had found his wife lacking in sympathy and understanding, and that this discovery was all the more painful because Milton had held, and still held, so high an ideal of what marriage should be. His disappointed love may have been made harder to bear by the thought that the purity and faith of his youth (he was now thirty-four) had not availed him in the choice of a wife. We cannot know much more than the fact of this hard experience, and that Milton was nevertheless ready to be reconciled to his wife when she sought reconciliation. But everything which enters into a poet's inner life must affect in some way his capacity for poetry; and it is safe to say that Milton's first marriage, little as we can know, or may wish to know, concerning it, was of a kind to confirm him in a certain severity of moral judgement.

Certainly an unlucky marriage must have limited Milton's direct knowledge and experience of human love. What did it do for his imaginative vision? When we read the great hymn to nuptial love in Book Four of *Paradise Lost*, and the description of the relationship between Adam and Eve, both before the Fall and in the scene of reconciliation which follows, we may doubt whether Milton's capacity for tenderness and for imaginative understanding was much narrowed: it may have been increased and deepened. After all, a poet who finds a difference between the two worlds of imagination and reality undergoes an experience which is itself twofold: if reality seems imperfect, it is surely because imagination is so rich. Milton's experience could therefore yield him either the tenderness of his passages of love and forgiveness; or on the other hand, Adam's bitter prophecy of the misery mankind will suffer through the love of women, Samson's obdurate rejection of his 'traitress' Dalila, and the remarks of Samson's friends on the moral inferiority of women to men. All these passages form part of great and magnificently organized works of art, in which much else finds a place. If Milton's personal experience in love and marriage had not been what it was, these great works might have been given a different emphasis, might have expressed a wider range of feeling. But if Milton had not been a great creative artist, if he had not been able to transform his own experience of life and make it part of a far-reaching vision, none of his personal experiences would have been of any use to him, or of any interest to us.

Samson Agonistes must be therefore seen as a self-sufficient work of art, before we can see how it also conveys Milton's view of his own life. He chose the Hebrew champion, whose mighty strength was given by God for the liberation of His people, as a fitting parallel to himself, his intellectual prowess dedicated to the achievement of truth and faith by his country. The seeming failure of Samson's mission, partly through the unworthiness of those for whom he laboured; his 'lot unfortunate in nuptial choice'; his overthrow, his blindness: all these features of the story could draw upon deep springs of personal emotion. But the analogy cannot be pressed at all points. How accurately can Mary Powell, apparently a placid English gentlewoman, be said to be represented by the cruel and treacherous Dalila? Is Samson's captivity, 'eyeless in Gaza at the mill with slaves', a close parallel to Milton's life in London under Charles II? And how precise an emblem is Samson's victorious death, the self-destruction entailed in the destruction of his enemies? No doubt Milton could feel that in the end he himself had triumphed; but it was a moral and intellectual victory, consisting as it did in his resurgence as the poet of *Paradise Lost*.

And it is the moral triumph, the survival of faith, which is the true subject of *Samson*. The poem is perhaps Milton's most convincing presentation of the theme of Temptation, everywhere to be found in his work and his thought. *Paradise Lost* showed human weakness tempted and falling. When he wished to show in *Paradise Regain'd* how God redeemed man, Milton chose an unusual aspect of the life of Christ, the Temptation in the Wilderness. In *Samson Agonistes* the hero's life and death include both Fall and Redemption; and redemption comes, as in *Paradise Regain'd*, through temptations overcome. Samson has betrayed his mission by yielding to sensuality and frivolity, laying himself open to a woman's guile: defeat and slavery have followed. His resurgence is achieved by his victory over temptation in various forms. Material baits are offered, but the true trial is spiritual. He rejects Manoa's care and Dalila's advances, both of which seem to hold out some hope for his future welfare; but above all he resists the temptation to blame anyone but himself: he has deserved his punishment, and will endure it. To try to evade it would be to deny, by implication, the justice of God's ways with men. By standing firm against these trials from without and from within, Samson is regenerated, and fulfils the purpose of his life by his inspired death.

By such inward issues the apparently slight plot is charged with dramatic tension. Dr. Johnson was strangely blind to the inner meaning of the play when he declared: 'the poem ... has a beginning and an end which *Aristotle* himself could not have disapproved; but it must be allowed to want a middle, since nothing passes between the first act and the last, that either hastens or delays the death of *Samson*.'[1] This is to miss, or to dismiss, the bearing of the various episodes on the hero's changing state of mind; and from what but from the hero's final state of mind does the catastrophe spring? The final act is foreshadowed by his unexpected decision about displaying his strength to the Philistines.[2] Milton makes it clear in his presentation of it that this change of mind is not related to any change in the outward situation. He also brings it out in the Argument: 'at length persuaded inwardly that this was from God, he yields to go along.'[3] God has sent a special inspiration to Samson, both here and immediately before the final deed.[4] But this inspiration would not have been granted if Samson had not been in a fit state to receive it. The preceding episodes have shown the preparation required: Samson has been tested

[1] *The Rambler*, No. 139.
[3] See p. 22.
[2] See ll. 1381–9 and n.
[4] See ll. 1636–8.

and found ready to submit to what God wills. The outcome
is no doubt unexpected: by accepting his apparent frustra-
tion, Samson becomes capable once more of heroic action.
But if this is ironical, it is no more so than the action as a
whole, which is pervaded with a dramatic irony that gives
it further point.[1]

The religion of the Old Testament moves powerfully
throughout the poem. The Book of Job had been present to
Milton's mind in writing *Paradise Regain'd*; but the story of
Samson, as Milton interprets it, is even closer to Job's trials
and affirmations. Milton's mind is steeped not only in the
faith of the Old Testament, but in Jewish history and
archaeology: Palestine is a vivid geographical reality in his
mind's eye, with its coastal plains, its hills and cities and
roads, and its wider setting of desert and sea. But above all
he feels intensely the fierce austerity of Hebrew religion, its
hatred of the idolatrous cults which surrounded it. The
idolatry of the Philistines is for him a symbol of the 'formal'
Christianity, whether Roman or Anglican, which he longed
for England to repudiate: the God of Israel triumphant over
Dagon displays the triumph of true religion, purified of all
but spiritual motives.

These religious implications mean that, while Milton
looked to Aeschylus, Sophocles, and Euripides for the form
of his drama, he did not try to write a tragedy of human life
as the Greeks saw it.[2] He had plainly asserted the superiority
of Christian and Hebrew religion over Greek thought in
Paradise Regain'd;[3] and he believed of course that his own
religion must give him an advantage even when he sought

[1] See E. M. W. Tillyard, *Milton* (London, 1930), p. 343.
[2] The relation of *Samson Agonistes* to Greek dramatic form is discussed
in the notes to Milton's preface, pp. 91–94 below.
[3] Book IV, ll. 285–364.

to follow Greek poetic achievements.[1] We need feel no
surprise when classical scholars tell us, as Sir Richard Jebb
did in a famous lecture, that '*Samson Agonistes* is a great
poem; it is also a noble drama. . . . But neither as poem nor
as drama is it Hellenic.'[2] Nor do we need to feel that this
observation in some way slights Milton's tragedy. How
should a boldly independent English Puritan of the seventeenth century, re-creating for his own purposes a story
from ancient Jewish literature, be expected also to convey
the vision of human life expressed in Athens in the fifth
century B.C.?

Yet Athens, which knew nothing of Christ or Israel,
gave Milton a poetic form which fits his thought. Milton's
religion is full of intellectual daring. His Christianity has
emerged from the Reformation and the Revival of Learn-
ing: it is a faith which has taken account of the Greek and
Roman moral philosophies which were then studied afresh,
and it can confidently make use of the methods of Attic
drama, which had also in its way expressed the philosophic
tendency of the Greek mind.[3]

It may, however, be suggested that, if *Samson Agonistes*
remains the most successful re-creation of Greek tragic
drama in our language, that is not only because Milton was

[1] He wrote in 1641 of his hope that 'what the greatest and choycest wits
of *Athens* . . . did for their country, I in my proportion with this over and
above of being a Christian, might doe for mine' (*The Reason of Church-
Government*, *Complete Prose Works*, Yale, vol. i, p. 812).

[2] '*Samson Agonistes* and the Hellenic Drama', *Proceedings of the British
Academy*, vol. iii (1907–8), p. 348.

[3] The discussion of 'Hellenism' and 'Hebraism' in *Samson Agonistes*
concerns the spirit of the poem. No one denies that Milton succeeded in
following the *form* of Greek drama. The controversy is therefore on the
difference between the Greek conception of human destiny, and that found
in Milton. The most useful contribution is 'The Greek Spirit in Milton's
Samson Agonistes', by W. R. Parker, in *Essays and Studies*, vol. xx (1935),
pp. 21–44.

a supreme poetic artist: it may also be because the intensity of his religious convictions gave his tragedy a quality which later attempts to follow Greek tragedy, like Swinburne's, have usually lacked—a seriousness which is related to the point of view of the Attic dramatists.

To many readers the religious fervour of *Samson Agonistes* may seem to have narrowed its imaginative scope, giving the poem an almost forbidding degree of austerity; and indeed the peculiar hardness and concentration of purpose which are a part of Milton's greatness of character, here find their plainest poetic equivalent. But the grimness of *Samson* is the result of a deliberate choice of position, of theme and treatment; and if we are to appreciate the poem we must learn to appreciate, among other things, the beauty of moral severity. Intransigence of judgement, firmness of faith, the acceptance of both action and suffering, are themselves moving and beautiful. Milton's ideal of 'heroic' poetry takes these things as its foundation, and we cannot understand it without entering into their spirit.

Of that sort of Dramatic Poem which is call'd Tragedy

Τραγῳδία μίμησις πράξεως σπουδαίας ... δι'ἐλέου καὶ φόβον περαίνουσα τὴν τῶν τοιόυτων παθημάτων κάθαρσιν.

ARISTOTLE, *Poet.* vi.

Tragoedia est imitatio actionis seriae ... per misericordiam et metum perficiens talium affectuum lustrationem.

TRAGEDY, as it was anciently composed, hath been ever held the gravest, moralest, and most profitable of all other Poems: therefore said by *Aristotle* to be of power by raising pity and fear, or terror, to purge the mind of those and such like passions, that is, to temper and reduce them to just 5 measure with a kind of delight, stirr'd up by reading or seeing those passions well imitated. Nor is Nature wanting in her own effects to make good his assertion: for so in Physic things of melancholic hue and quality are used against melancholy, sour against sour, salt to remove salt 10 humours. Hence Philosophers and other gravest Writers, as *Cicero*, *Plutarch* and others, frequently cite out of Tragic Poets, both to adorn and illustrate their discourse. The Apostle *Paul* himself thought it not unworthy to insert a verse of *Euripides* into the Text of Holy Scripture, 1 *Cor.* 15 15. 33; and *Paræus* commenting on the *Revelation*, divides the whole Book as a Tragedy, into Acts distinguished each by a Chorus of Heavenly Harpings and Song between. Heretofore Men in highest dignity have labour'd not a little to be thought able to compose a Tragedy. Of that 20 honour *Dionysius* the elder was no less ambitious, than before of his attaining to the Tyranny. *Augustus Cæsar* also had begun his *Ajax*, but unable to please his own judgement with what he had begun, left it unfinished. *Seneca* the

Philosopher is by some thought the Author of those 25
Tragedies (at least the best of them) that go under that
name. *Gregory Nazianzen* a Father of the Church, thought
it not unbeseeming the sanctity of his person to write a
Tragedy, which he entitled, *Christ Suffering*. This is mention'd to vindicate Tragedy from the small esteem, or 30
rather infamy, which in the account of many it undergoes
at this day with other common Interludes; happening
through the Poets' error of intermixing Comic stuff with
Tragic sadness and gravity; or introducing trivial and
vulgar persons, which by all judicious hath been counted 35
absurd; and brought in without discretion, corruptly to
gratify the people. And though ancient Tragedy use no
Prologue, yet using sometimes, in case of self-defence, or
explanation, that which *Martial* calls an Epistle; in behalf of
this Tragedy coming forth after the ancient manner, much 40
different from what among us passes for best, thus much
before-hand may be Epistled; that *Chorus* is here introduced after the Greek manner, not ancient only but modern,
and still in use among the *Italians*. In the modelling therefore of this Poem, with good reason, the Ancients and 45
Italians are rather follow'd, as of much more authority and
fame. The measure of Verse used in the Chorus is of all
sorts, call'd by the Greeks *Monostrophic*, or rather *Apolelymenon*, without regard had to *Strophe*, *Antistrophe* or *Epode*,
which were a kind of Stanza's framed only for the Music, 50
then used with the Chorus that sung; not essential to the
Poem, and therefore not material; or being divided into
Stanza's or Pauses, they may be call'd *Allæostropha*. Division
into Act and Scene referring chiefly to the Stage (to which
this work never was intended) is here omitted. It suffices if 55
the whole Drama be found not produced beyond the
fifth Act.

Of the style and uniformity, and that commonly call'd the Plot, whether intricate or explicit, which is nothing indeed but such economy, or disposition of the fable as 60 may stand best with verisimilitude and decorum, they only will best judge who are not unacquainted with *Aeschylus*, *Sophocles*, and *Euripides*, the three Tragic Poets unequall'd yet by any, and the best rule to all who endeavour to write Tragedy. The circumscription of time wherein the whole 65 Drama begins and ends, is according to ancient rule, and best example, within the space of 24 hours.

The ARGUMENT

SAMSON *made Captive, Blind, and now in the Prison at* Gaza, *there to labour as in a common work-house, on a Festival day, in the general cessation from labour, comes forth into the open Air, to a place nigh, somewhat retired, there to sit awhile and bemoan his condition. Where he happens at length to be visited by certain friends and equals of his tribe, which make the Chorus, who seek to comfort him what they can; then by his old Father* Manoa, *who endeavours the like, and withal tells him his purpose to procure his liberty by ransom; lastly, that this Feast was proclaim'd by the* Philistines *as a day of Thanksgiving for their deliverance from the hands of* Samson, *which yet more troubles him.* Manoa *then departs to prosecute his endeavour with the* Philistian *Lords for* Samson's *redemption; who in the meanwhile is visited by other persons; and lastly by a public Officer to require his coming to the Feast before the Lords and People, to play or show his strength in their presence. He at first refuses, dismissing the public Officer with absolute denial to come; at length persuaded inwardly that this was from God, he yields to go along with him, who came now the second time with great threatenings to fetch him. The Chorus yet remaining on the place,* Manoa *returns full of joyful hope, to procure ere long his Son's deliverance: in the midst of which discourse an* Ebrew *comes in haste confusedly at first, and afterward more distinctly, relating the Catastrophe, what* Samson *had done to the* Philistines, *and by accident to himself; wherewith the Tragedy ends.*

THE PERSONS

Samson.	Dalila *his Wife*.	Messenger.
Manoa *the Father of* Samson.	Harapha *of* Gath.	Chorus *of* Danites.
	Public Officer.	

The Scene before the Prison in Gaza.

SAMSON AGONISTES

Samson. A little onward lend thy guiding hand
  To these dark steps, a little further on;
  For yonder bank hath choice of Sun or shade.
  There I am wont to sit, when any chance
  Relieves me from my task of servile toil,
  Daily in the common Prison else enjoin'd me,
  Where I a Pris'ner chain'd, scarce freely draw
  The air imprison'd also, close and damp,
  Unwholesome draught: but here I feel amends,
  The breath of Heav'n fresh-blowing, pure and sweet,   10
  With day-spring born; here leave me to respire.
  This day a solemn Feast the people hold
  To *Dagon* their Sea-Idol, and forbid
  Laborious works; unwillingly this rest
  Their Superstition yields me: hence with leave
  Retiring from the popular noise, I seek
  This unfrequented place to find some ease,
  Ease to the body some, none to the mind
  From restless thoughts, that like a deadly swarm
  Of Hornets arm'd, no sooner found alone,   20
  But rush upon me thronging, and present
  Times past, what once I was, and what am now.
  O wherefore was my birth from Heav'n foretold
  Twice by an Angel, who at last in sight

2 *these dark steps*: i.e. the steps which Samson takes, 'dark' because he is
blind.   6 *else*: otherwise.   *enjoin'd me*: imposed on me (see 1342).
9 *draught*: air drawn, or breathed, in.   11 *day-spring*: early dawn.
respire: breathe, i.e. rest.   16 *the popular noise*: the noise made by the
people.   19–21 'thoughts, that rush upon me like a swarm of hornets,
as soon as I find myself alone'.

Of both my Parents all in flames ascended
From off the Altar, where an Off'ring burn'd,
As in a fiery column charioting
His Godlike presence, and from some great act
Or benefit reveal'd to *Abraham*'s race?
Why was my breeding order'd and prescribed   30
As of a person separate to God,
Design'd for great exploits; if I must die
Betray'd, Captived, and both my Eyes put out,
Made of my Enemies the scorn and gaze;
To grind in Brazen Fetters under task
With this Heav'n-gifted strength? O glorious strength
Put to the labour of a Beast, debased
Lower than bondslave! Promise was that I
Should *Israel* from *Philistian* yoke deliver;
Ask for this great Deliverer now, and find him   40
Eyeless in *Gaza* at the Mill with slaves,
Himself in bonds under *Philistian* yoke;
Yet stay, let me not rashly call in doubt
Divine Prediction; what if all foretold
Had been fulfill'd but through mine own default?
Whom have I to complain of but myself?
Who this high gift of strength committed to me,
In what part lodged, how easily bereft me,
Under the Seal of silence could not kéep,
But weakly to a woman must reveal it   50

27 *charioting*: riding as if in a chariot.   28–29 *and from some great act . . .
reveal'd*: 'and as if he had revealed some great act'.   30 *breeding*: up-
bringing.   31 *separate*: set apart.   34 *gaze*: spectacle, or gazing
stock.   35 *under task*: allotted a certain portion of labour.   38
Promise was: it was promised.   45 *but through*: except for.   47–49
'who could not be silent about where the gift committed to me was
lodged and how easily it could be taken from me'.   48 *bereft me*: taken
from me.

O'ercome with importunity and tears.
O impotence of mind, in body strong!
But what is strength without a double share
Of wisdom? vast, unwieldy, burdensome,
Proudly secure, yet liable to fall
By weakest subtleties, not made to rule,
But to subserve where wisdom bears command.
God, when he gave me strength, to show withal
How slight the gift was, hung it in my Hair.
But peace, I must not quarrel with the will   60
Of highest dispensation, which herein
Haply had ends above my reach to know:
Suffices that to me strength is my bane,
And proves the source of all my miseries;
So many, and so huge, that each apart
Would ask a life to wail, but chief of all,
O loss of sight, of thee I most complain!
Blind among enemies, O worse than chains,
Dungeon, or beggary, or decrepit age!
Light the prime work of God to me is extinct,   70
And all her various objects of delight
Annull'd, which might in part my grief have eased,
Inferior to the vilest now become
Of man or worm; the vilest here excel me,
They creep, yet see, I dark in light exposed
To daily fraud, contempt, abuse and wrong,
Within doors, or without, still as a fool,
In power of others, never in my own;

55 *secure*: careless, heedless of danger (the literal Latin sense, *sine cura*).
56 *By weakest subtleties*: by cunning of even the weakest kind.   57
subserve: serve as a subordinate.   60 *quarrel with*: find fault with.
63 *Suffices that*: it suffices me to know that.   66 *ask*: demand, need.
70 *prime*: first.   *extinct*: extinguished (the Latin sense).   77 *still as a*
fool: always in the position of a fool, i.e. easily deceived.

Scarce half I seem to live, dead more than half.
O dark, dark, dark, amid the blaze of noon,   80
Irrecoverably dark, total Eclipse
Without all hope of day!
O first created Beam, and thou great Word,
Let there be light, and light was over all;
Why am I thus bereaved thy prime decree?
The Sun to me is dark
And silent as the Moon,
When she deserts the night
Hid in her vacant interlunar cave.
Since light so necessary is to life,   90
And almost life itself, if it be true
That light is in the Soul,
She all in every part; why was the sight
To such a tender ball as th' eye confined,
So obvious and so easy to be quench'd,
And not as feeling through all parts diffused,
That she might look at will through every pore?
Then had I not been thus exiled from light;
As in the land of darkness yet in light,
To live a life half dead, a living death,   100
And buried; but O yet more miserable!
Myself my Sepulchre, a moving Grave,
Buried, yet not exempt
By privilege of death and burial
From worst of other evils, pains and wrongs;
But made hereby obnoxious more
To all the miseries of life,
Life in captivity
Among inhuman foes.

89 *interlunar*: between moons.   95 *obvious*: exposed.   96 *as*:
like.   106 *obnoxious*: exposed, liable.

But who are these? for with joint pace I hear   110
The tread of many feet steering this way;
Perhaps my enemies who come to stare
At my affliction, and perhaps to insult,
Their daily practice to afflict me more.

Chorus. This, this is he; softly awhile,
  Let us not break in upon him;
  O change beyond report, thought, or belief!
  See how he lies at random, carelessly diffused,
  With languish'd head unpropp'd,
  As one past hope, abandon'd   120
  And by himself given over;
  In slavish habit, ill-fitted weeds
  O'erworn and soil'd;
  Or do my eyes misrepresent? Can this be he,
  That Heroic, that Renown'd,
  Irresistible *Samson*? whom unarm'd
  No strength of man, or fiercest wild beast could withstand;
  Who tore the Lion, as the Lion tears the Kid,
  Ran on embattled Armies clad in Iron,
  And weaponless himself,   130
  Made Arms ridiculous, useless the forgery
  Of brazen shield and spear, the hammer'd Cuirass,
  Chalybean temper'd steel, and frock of mail
  Adamantean Proof;
  But safest he who stood aloof,
  When insupportably his foot advanced,

111 *steering*: directing their course.   113 *insult*: exult.   118
diffused: spread loosely, sprawled.   119 *languish'd*: relaxed, drooping.
unpropp'd: not supported in any way.   122 *habit*: dress.   *weeds*:
clothes.   129 *embattled*: drawn up in battle formation.   131 *forgery*: something made by forging.   134 *Adamantean Proof*: *either* proof
against adamantean weapons *or* proof as being itself adamant.   136 in-
supportably: irresistibly.

In scorn of their proud arms and warlike tools,
Spurn'd them to death by Troops. The bold *Ascalonite*
Fled from his Lion ramp, old Warriors turn'd
Their plated backs under his heel;   140
Or grov'lling soil'd their crested helmets in the dust.
Then with what trivial weapon came to hand,
The Jaw of a dead Ass, his sword of bone,
A thousand fore-skins fell, the flower of *Palestine*
In *Ramath-lechi* famous to this day:
Then by main force pull'd up, and on his shoulders bore
The Gates of *Azza*, Post, and massy Bar
Up to the Hill by *Hebron*, seat of Giants old,
No journey of a Sabbath day, and loaded so;
Like whom the Gentiles feign to bear up Heav'n.   150
Which shall I first bewail,
Thy Bondage or lost Sight,
Prison within Prison
Inseparably dark?
Thou art become (O worst imprisonment!)
The Dungeon of thyself; thy Soul
(Which Men enjoying sight oft without cause complain)
Imprison'd now indeed,
In real darkness of the body dwells,
Shut up from outward light   160
To incorporate with gloomy night;
For inward light alas
Puts forth no visual beam.
ʹO mirror of our fickle state,
Since man on earth unparallel'd!

137 *tools*: weapons.   139 *ramp*: spring, leap.   140 *plated*:
armoured.   144 *fore-skins*: i.e. Philistines.   157 *complain*: complain of, lament.   161 *incorporate*: dwell together in one body.
164 *mirror*: reflection, picture.   165 'unparalleled since man came on
earth'.

The rarer thy example stands,
By how much from the top of wondrous glory,
Strongest of mortal men,
To lowest pitch of abject fortune thou art fall'n.
For him I reckon not in high estate   170
Whom long descent of birth
Or the sphere of fortune raises;
But thee whose strength, while virtue was her mate
Might have subdued the Earth,
Universally crown'd with highest praises.

Samson. I hear the sound of words, their sense the air
  Dissolves unjointed ere it reach my ear.

Chorus. He speaks, let us draw nigh. Matchless in might,
  The glory late of *Israel*, now the grief;
  We come thy friends and neighbours not unknown   180
  From *Eshtaol* and *Zora*'s fruitful Vale
  To visit or bewail thee, or if better,
  Counsel or Consolation we may bring,
  Salve to thy Sores; apt words have power to swage
  The tumours of a troubled mind,
  And are as Balm to fester'd wounds.

Samson. Your coming, Friends, revives me, for I learn
  Now of my own experience, not by talk,
  How counterfeit a coin they are who friends
  Bear in their Superscription (of the most   190
  I would be understood); in prosperous days
  They swarm, but in adverse withdraw their head

173. 'But thee I do reckon, or should have reckoned, in high estate,
whose. . . .'   177 *unjointed*: disconnected.   179 *The glory late*:
lately the glory.   184 *swage*: assuage, soothe.   189–90 *who friends
Bear in their Superscription*: who are outwardly or nominally friends.
190–1 *of the most I would be understood*: 'I wish to be understood to speak
of most people (but not you)'.

Not to be found, though sought. Ye see, O friends,
How many evils have enclosed me round;
Yet that which was the worst now least afflicts me,
Blindness, for had I sight, confused with shame,
How could I once look up, or heave the head,
Who like a foolish Pilot have shipwreck'd
My Vessel trusted to me from above,
Gloriously rigg'd; and for a word, a tear,   200
Fool, have divulged the secret gift of God
To a deceitful Woman: tell me Friends,
Am I not sung and proverb'd for a Fool
In every street, do they not say, how well
Are come upon him his deserts? yet why?
Immeasurable strength they might behold
In me, of wisdom nothing more than mean;
This with the other should, at least, have pair'd,
These two proportion'd ill drove me transverse.

Chorus. Tax not divine disposal, wisest Men   210
   Have err'd, and by bad Women been deceived;
   And shall again, pretend they ne'er so wise.
   Deject not then so overmuch thyself,
   Who hast of sorrow thy full load besides;
   Yet truth to say, I oft have heard men wonder
   Why thou shouldst wed *Philistian* women rather
   Than of thine own Tribe fairer, or as fair,
   At least of thy own Nation, and as noble.

   197 *heave the head*: lift up my head.   203 *proverb'd*: made a by-word,
or common example.   207 *mean*: average.   208 *pair'd*: made a
pair, i.e. been equally proportioned.   209 *drove me transverse*: drove
me out of my course.   210 *Tax*: charge with a fault, take to task.
divine disposal: God's control of events.   212 *pretend they ne'er so wise*:
however wise they claim to be.   213 *Deject*: cast down.   217–18
'Than equally beautiful, or more beautiful, women from your own tribe, or
at least from your own people, and of the same social standing as yourself.'

Samson. The first I saw at *Timna*, and she pleased
  Me, not my parents, that I sought to wed   220
  The daughter of an Infidel: they knew not
  That what I motion'd was of God; I knew
  From intimate impulse, and therefore urged
  The Marriage on; that by occasion hence
  I might begin *Israel*'s Deliverance,
  The work to which I was divinely call'd;
  She proving false, the next I took to Wife
  (O that I never had! fond wish too late)
  Was in the Vale of *Sorec*, *Dalila*,
  That specious Monster, my accomplish'd snare.   230
  I thought it lawful from my former act,
  And the same end; still watching to oppress
  Israel's oppressors: of what now I suffer
  She was not the prime cause, but I myself,
  Who vanquish'd with a peal of words (O weakness!)
  Gave up my fort of silence to a Woman.

Chorus. In seeking just occasion to provoke
  The *Philistine*, thy Country's Enemy,
  Thou never wast remiss, I bear thee witness:
  Yet *Israel* still serves with all his Sons.   240

Samson. That fault I take not on me, but transfer

220 *not my parents, that I sought to wed*: it did not please my parents that
I sought to wed.   222 *motion'd*: proposed, set on foot.   223
intimate: inward.   224 *that by occasion hence*: in order that from this
an opportunity might come.   226 *divinely*: by God or by Heaven.
228 *fond*: foolish, vain.   229 *Dalila*: accent 'Dálila'.   230 *specious*:
fair-seeming, but deceptive.   *accomplish'd*: skilled, or complete.   231–2
'I thought it lawful because I had done the same thing before, and because
my object was the same (to take action against the Philistines).'   235
peal: din.   236 *my fort of silence*: the stronghold or strength I possessed
as long as I remained silent.   237 *provoke*: challenge (the Latin sense).
240 *still serves*: is still subjected to the Philistines.

On *Israel*'s Governors, and Heads of Tribes,
Who seeing those great acts which God had done
Singly by me against their Conquerors
Acknowledged not, or not at all consider'd
Deliverance offer'd: I on th' other side
Used no ambition to commend my deeds,
The deeds themselves, though mute, spoke loud the doer;
But they persisted deaf, and would not seem
To count them things worth notice, till at length   250
Their Lords the *Philistines* with gather'd powers
Enter'd *Judea* seeking me, who then
Safe to the rock of *Etham* was retired,
Not flying, but fore-casting in what place
To set upon them, what advantaged best.
Meanwhile the men of *Judah* to prevent
The harass of their Land, beset me round;
I willingly on some conditions came
Into their hands, and they as gladly yield me
To the uncircumcised a welcome prey,   260
Bound with two cords; but cords to me were threads
Touch'd with the flame: on their whole Host I flew
Unarm'd, and with a trivial weapon fell'd
Their choicest youth; they only lived who fled.
Had *Judah* that day join'd, or one whole Tribe,
They had by this possess'd the Towers of *Gath*,
And lorded over them whom now they serve;
But what more oft in Nations grown corrupt,
And by their vices brought to servitude,
Than to love Bondage more than Liberty,   270

247 *ambition*: soliciting or canvassing (Latin *ambitus*, 'going round' to
collect votes or support).   249 *they persisted deaf*: they remained
obstinately deaf.   263 *a trivial weapon*: i.e. the ass's jawbone.   267
lorded: ruled.   268 *But what more oft*: but what is more common.

Bondage with ease than strenuous Liberty;
And to despise, or envy, or suspect
Whom God hath of his special favour raised
As their Deliverer? if he aught begin,
How frequent to desert him, and at last
To heap ingratitude on worthiest deeds?

Chorus. Thy words to my remembrance bring
  How *Succoth* and the Fort of *Penuel*
  Their great Deliverer contemn'd,
  The matchless *Gideon* in pursuit   280
  Of *Madian* and her vanquish'd Kings:
  And how ingrateful *Ephraim*
  Had dealt with *Jephtha*, who by argument,
  Not worse than by his shield and spear
  Defended *Israel* from the *Ammonite*,
  Had not his prowess quell'd their pride
  In that sore battle when so many died
  Without Reprieve adjudged to death,
  For want of well pronouncing *Shibboleth*.

Samson. Of such examples add me to the roll;   290
  Me easily indeed mine may neglect,
  But God's proposed deliverance not so.

Chorus. Just are the ways of God,
  And justifiable to Men;
  Unless there be who think not God at all.
  If any be, they walk obscure;
  For of such Doctrine never was there School,

275 *How frequent to desert him*: how frequently they desert him.   282
ingrateful: ungrateful.   291-2 'My people may neglect me easily
enough, but they cannot so easily neglect God's plans for their liberation.'
295 'Unless there be some who think there is no God at all'.

But the heart of the Fool,
And no man therein Doctor but himself.
  Yet more there be who doubt his ways not just,   300
As to his own edicts found contradicting,
Then give the reins to wand'ring thought,
Regardless of his glory's diminution;
Till by their own perplexities involved
They ravel more, still less resolved,
But never find self-satisfying solution.
  As if they would confine th' interminable,
And tie him to his own prescript,
Who made our Laws to bind us, not himself,
And hath full right to exempt   310
Whom so it pleases him by choice
From National obstriction, without taint
Of sin, or legal debt;
For with his own Laws he can best dispense.
  He would not else who never wanted means,
Nor in respect of the enemy just cause
To set his people free,
Have prompted this Heroic *Nazarite*,
Against his vow of strictest purity,
To seek in marriage that fallacious Bride,   320
Unclean, unchaste.
  Down Reason then, at least vain reasonings down,
Though Reason here aver
That moral verdit quits her of unclean:

299 *Doctor*: a qualified teacher (the Latin sense).   300 'But there are
more people who doubt whether his ways are just.'   301 *edicts*: accent
'edícts'.   305 *ravel*: become tangled, perplexed.   *resolved*: decided.
307 *th' interminable*: the infinite, i.e. God.   312 *National obstriction*:
moral or legal obligation on the whole people.   320 *fallacious*: deceitful.   322 *Down Reason then*: let Reason then submit.   324 *verdit*:
verdict.   *quits*: acquits.

Unchaste was subsequent, her stain not his.
  But see here comes thy reverend Sire
With careful step, Locks white as down,
Old *Manoa*: advise
Forthwith how thou oughtst to receive him.

Samson. Ay me, another inward grief, awaked   330
  With mention of that name renews th' assault.

Manoa. Brethren and men of *Dan*, for such ye seem,
  Though in this uncouth place: if old respect,
  As I suppose, towards your once gloried friend,
  My Son now Captive, hither hath inform'd
  Your younger feet, while mine cast back with age
  Came lagging after; say if he be here.

Chorus. As signal now in low dejected state,
  As erst in highest, behold him where he lies.

Manoa. O miserable change! is this the man,   340
  That invincible *Samson*, far renown'd,
  The dread of *Israel*'s foes, who with a strength
  Equivalent to Angels' walk'd their streets,
  None offering fight; who single combatant
  Duell'd their Armies rank'd in proud array,
  Himself an Army, now unequal match
  To save himself against a coward arm'd
  At one spear's length. O ever failing trust

325 *Unchaste was subsequent*: her unchastity followed marriage.   327
careful: weighed down with care.   328 *Manoa*: accent 'Mánoa'.
advise: take thought.   333 *uncouth*: unknown, strange.   334 *gloried*:
surrounded by glory.   335 *inform'd*: guided or moved.   338 *signal*:
conspicuous, notable.   *dejected*: cast down.   345 *Duell'd*: fought as
man to man; i.e. he was as strong as the whole army he fought.   348
At one spear's length: even at close quarters.

In mortal strength! and oh what not in man
Deceivable and vain! Nay what thing good   350
Pray'd for, but often proves our woe, our bane?
I pray'd for Children, and thought barrenness
In wedlock a reproach; I gain'd a Son,
And such a Son as all Men hail'd me happy;
Who would be now a Father in my stead?
O wherefore did God grant me my request,
And as a blessing with such pomp adorn'd?
Why are his gifts desirable, to tempt
Our earnest Prayers, then giv'n with solemn hand
As Graces, draw a Scorpion's tail behind?   360
For this did the Angel twice descend? for this
Ordain'd thy nurture holy, as of a Plant
Select, and Sacred, Glorious for a while,
The miracle of men: then in an hour
Ensnared, assaulted, overcome, led bound,
Thy foes' derision, Captive, Poor, and Blind
Into a Dungeon thrust, to work with Slaves?
Alas methinks whom God hath chosen once
To worthiest deeds, if he through frailty err,
He should not so o'erwhelm, and as a thrall   370
Subject him to so foul indignities,
Be it but for honour's sake of former deeds.

Samson. Appoint not heav'nly disposition, Father,
Nothing of all these evils hath befall'n me

349–50 'what is there in man that is not deceivable and vain?' *De-*
ceivable: deceptive.   351 *Pray'd for*: i.e. is there prayed for.   354
as: that.   357 *pomp*: solemnity.   360 *Graces*: favours (Latin
gratiae).   364 *The miracle of men*: the admiration of all, as a wonder.
366 *Thy foes' derision*: an object of laughter to thy foes.   370 *thrall*:
one in bondage, a serf or slave.   373 *Either* 'Do not prescribe a set
course of action for God' *or* 'Do not blame, or call into question, God's
actions'.

But justly; I myself have brought them on,
Sole Author I, sole cause: if aught seem vile,
As vile hath been my folly, who have profaned
The mystery of God giv'n me under pledge
Of vow, and have betray'd it to a woman,
A *Canaanite*, my faithless enemy.   380
This well I knew, nor was at all surprised,
But warn'd by oft experience: did not she
Of *Timna* first betray me, and reveal
The secret wrested from me in her highth
Of Nuptial Love profess'd, carrying it straight
To them who had corrupted her, my Spies,
And Rivals? In this other was there found
More Faith? who also in her prime of love,
Spousal embraces, vitiated with Gold,
Though offer'd only, by the scent conceived   390
Her spurious first-born, Treason against me?
Thrice she assay'd with flattering prayers and sighs,
And amorous reproaches to win from me
My capital secret, in what part my strength
Lay stored, in what part summ'd, that she might know:
Thrice I deluded her, and turn'd to sport
Her importunity, each time perceiving
How openly, and with what impudence
She purposed to betray me, and (which was worse
Than undissembled hate) with what contempt   400
She sought to make me Traitor to myself;

384–5 *in her highth Of Nuptial Love profess'd*: at the height of her
professions of wedded love.   389 *Spousal embraces*: (In) her (first) embraces as a wife.   *vitiated*: tainted, corrupted.   389–91 'seduced by
the mere offer of money (*the scent*), conceived an illegitimate (*spurious*)
first-born child, and this child was treachery against me'.   392 *assay'd*:
tried.   394–5 *in what part . . . know*: so that she might learn in what
part of my body my strength was concentrated and kept.

Yet the fourth time, when must'ring all her wiles,
With blandish'd parleys, feminine assaults,
Tongue-batteries, she surceased not day nor night
To storm me over-watch'd, and wearied out,
At times when men seek most repose and rest,
I yielded, and unlock'd her all my heart,
Who with a grain of manhood well resolved
Might easily have shook off all her snares:
But foul effeminacy held me yoked   410
Her Bond-slave; O indignity, O blot
To Honour and Religion! servile mind
Rewarded well with servile punishment!
The base degree to which I now am fall'n,
These rags, this grinding, is not yet so base
As was my former servitude, ignoble,
Unmanly, ignominious, infamous,
True slavery, and that blindness worse than this,
That saw not how degenerately I served.

Manoa. I cannot praise thy Marriage choices, Son,   420
Rather approved them not; but thou didst plead
Divine impulsion prompting how thou mightst
Find some occasion to infest our Foes.
I state not that; this I am sure; our Foes
Found soon occasion thereby to make thee
Their Captive, and their triumph; thou the sooner
Temptation found'st, or over-potent charms

402 *must'ring*: gathering like troops.   403 *blandish'd parleys*: flattering
or soothing speeches.   404 *surceased*: came to a stop.   405
over-watch'd: tired out by having to keep awake.   408 *grain*: the
smallest measure of weight.   *well resolved*: fully determined.   421
Rather approved them not: on the contrary I never did approve of them.
423 *infest*: molest or attack.   424 *I state not that*: I do not bring that
into question.   *this I am sure*: I am sure of this.   426 *their triumph*: an
occasion for them to triumph.

To violate the sacred trust of silence
Deposited within thee; which to have kept
Tacit, was in thy power. True; and thou bear'st   430
Enough, and more, the burden of that fault;
Bitterly hast thou paid, and still art paying
That rigid score. A worse thing yet remains:
This day the *Philistines* a popular Feast
Here celebrate in *Gaza*; and proclaim
Great Pomp, and Sacrifice, and Praises loud
To *Dagon*, as their God who hath deliver'd
Thee *Samson* bound and blind into their hands,
Them out of thine, who slew'st them many a slain.
So *Dagon* shall be magnified, and God,   440
Besides whom is no God, compared with Idols,
Disglorified, blasphemed, and had in scorn
By th' Idolatrous rout amidst their wine;
Which to have come to pass by means of thee,
Samson, of all thy sufferings think the heaviest,
Of all reproach the most with shame that ever
Could have befall'n thee and thy Father's house.

Samson. Father, I do acknowledge and confess
  That I this honour, I this pomp have brought
  To *Dagon*, and advanced his praises high   450
  Among the Heathen round; to God have brought
  Dishonour, obloquy, and oped the mouths
  Of Idolists, and Atheists; have brought scandal

433 *rigid score*: unchanging fine or penalty.   434 *a popular Feast*:
a general holiday or festival.   436 *Pomp*: solemn festivity (Latin,
pompa, a festival procession).   441 *compared with*: put on an equal
footing with.   442 *Disglorified*: deprived of glory, dishonoured.
444 *Which to have come to pass*: and the fact that this has come to pass.
446 *Of all reproach the most with shame*: the most shameful of all reproaches.
452 *oped the mouths*: given occasion for triumphant talk.   453 *Idolists*:
idolaters.

To *Israel*, diffidence of God, and doubt
In feeble hearts, propense enough before
To waver, or fall off and join with Idols:
Which is my chief affliction, shame and sorrow,
The anguish of my Soul, that suffers not
Mine eye to harbour sleep, or thoughts to rest.
This only hope relieves me, that the strife   460
With me hath end; all the contest is now
'Twixt God and *Dagon*; *Dagon* hath presumed,
Me overthrown, to enter lists with God,
His deity comparing and preferring
Before the God of *Abraham*. He, be sure,
Will not connive, or linger, thus provoked,
But will arise and his great name assert:
Dagon must stoop, and shall ere long receive
Such a discomfit, as shall quite despoil him
Of all these boasted Trophies won on me,   470
And with confusion blank his Worshippers.

Manoa. With cause this hope relieves thee, and these words
I as a Prophecy receive: for God,
Nothing more certain, will not long defer
To vindicate the glory of his name
Against all competition, nor will long
Endure it, doubtful whether God be Lord, ₑ
Or *Dagon*. But for thee what shall be done?
Thou must not in the meanwhile here forgot
Lie in this miserable Loathsome plight   480
Neglected. I already have made way

    454 *diffidence of God*: distrust of, lack of faith in, God.   455 *propense*:
inclined, ready or willing.   456 *fall off*: default, desert the cause.
463 *enter lists with*: challenge.   466 *connive*: be long-suffering (lit.
wink, shut one's eyes).   469 *discomfit*: discomfiture, blow.   471
blank: blanch, turn pale.   477 *God*: i.e. Jehovah.

To some *Philistian* Lords, with whom to treat
About thy ransom: well they may by this
Have satisfied their utmost of revenge
By pains and slaveries, worse than death inflicted
On thee, who now no more canst do them harm.

Samson. Spare that proposal, Father, spare the trouble
  Of that solicitation; let me here,
  As I deserve, pay on my punishment;
  And expiate, if possible, my crime,   490
  Shameful garrulity. To have reveal'd
  Secrets of men, the secrets of a friend,
  How hainous had the fact been, how deserving
  Contempt, and scorn of all, to be excluded
  All friendship, and avoided as a blab,
  The mark of fool set on his front? But I
  God's counsel have not kept, his holy secret
  Presumptuously have publish'd, impiously,
  Weakly at least, and shamefully: a sin
  That Gentiles in their Parables condemn   500
  To their abyss and horrid pains confined.

Manoa. Be penitent and for thy fault contrite,
  But act not in thy own affliction, Son.
  Repent the sin, but if the punishment
  Thou canst avoid, self-preservation bids;
  Or th' execution leave to high disposal,

483 *by this*: by now.   484 *their utmost of revenge*: their fullest ven-
geance.   489 *pay on*: continue to pay.   493 *hainous*: hateful,
infamous.   *fact*: deed.   495 *blab*: a babbler or tell-tale.   496
front: forehead.   500–1 *condemn . . . confined*: condemn to be confined in the abyss they believe in, and suffer its dreadful torments.
505 *bids*: bids thee do so.   506 *to high disposal*: i.e. to God's
providence.

And let another hand, not thine, exact
Thy penal forfeit from thyself. Perhaps
God will relent, and quit thee all his debt;
Who evermore approves and more accepts   510
(Best pleased with humble and filial submission)
Him who imploring mercy sues for life,
Than who self-rigorous chooses death as due:
Which argues over-just, and self-displeased
For self-offence, more than for God offended.
Reject not then what offer'd means, who knows
But God hath set before us, to return thee
Home to thy country and his sacred house,
Where thou mayst bring thy off'rings, to avert
His further ire, with prayers and vows renew'd.   520

Samson. His pardon I implore; but as for life,
To what end should I seek it? when in strength
All mortals I excell'd, and great in hopes
With youthful courage and magnanimous thoughts
Of birth from Heav'n foretold and high exploits,
Full of divine instinct, after some proof
Of acts indeed heroic, far beyond
The Sons of *Anak*, famous now and blazed,
Fearless of danger, like a petty God
I walk'd about admired of all and dreaded   530
On hostile ground, none daring my affront:

507–8 *exact Thy penal forfeit*: exact from you the payment due as
punishment.   509 *quit thee all his debt*: remit the punishment you
owe him.   514–15 'Which (i.e. the demand for his own death)
indicates that the sinner is excessively scrupulous, and is more displeased
with himself for the wrong he has done himself than for the wrong he
has done to God.'   516–17 'Do not reject whatever opportunities
(*means*) are offered, which (who knows?) God may have set before us,
so that He may return thee', &c.   526 *divine instinct*: impulse or
prompting from God.   528 *blazed*: proclaimed as with a trumpet.

Then swoll'n with pride into the snare I fell
Of fair fallacious looks, venereal trains,
Soften'd with pleasure and voluptuous life;
At length to lay my head and hallow'd pledge
Of all my strength in the lascivious lap
Of a deceitful Concubine who shore me
Like a tame Wether, all my precious fleece,
Then turn'd me out ridiculous, despoil'd,
Shav'n, and disarm'd among my enemies.   540

Chorus. Desire of wine and all delicious drinks,
  Which many a famous Warrior overturns,
  Thou couldst repress, nor did the dancing Ruby
  Sparkling, out-pour'd, the flavour, or the smell,
  Or taste that cheers the heart of Gods and men,
  Allure thee from the cool Crystalline stream.

Samson. Wherever fountain or fresh current flow'd
  Against the Eastern ray, translucent, pure,
  With touch ætherial of Heav'n's fiery rod
  I drank, from the clear milky juice allaying   550
  Thirst, and refresh'd; nor envied them the grape
  Whose heads that turbulent liquor fills with fumes.

Chorus. O madness, to think use of strongest wines
  And strongest drinks our chief support of health,
  When God with these forbidd'n made choice to rear
  His mighty Champion, strong above compare,
  Whose drink was only from the liquid brook.

533 *venereal trains*: temptations of love.   537 *who shore me*: who
clipped from me.   538 *Wether*: a male sheep, especially one which
has been castrated.   543 *the dancing Ruby*: i.e. wine.   549 *ætherial*:
ethereal.   *Heav'n's fiery rod*: the sun's rays.   550 *the clear milky
juice*: water.   551 *refresh'd*: refreshed myself.   552 *that turbulent
liquor*: liquor causing confusion of mind, or other turbulence.   557
liquid: clear, transparent.

Samson. But what avail'd this temperance, not complete
   Against another object more enticing?
   What boots it at one gate to make defence,   560
   And at another to let in the foe
   Effeminately vanquish'd? by which means,
   Now blind, dishearten'd, shamed, dishonour'd, quell'd,
   To what can I be useful, wherein serve
   My Nation, and the work from Heav'n imposed,
   But to sit idle on the household hearth,
   A burdenous drone; to visitants a gaze,
   Or pitied object, these redundant locks
   Robustious to no purpose clust'ring down,
   Vain monument of strength; till length of years   570
   And sedentary numbness craze my limbs
   To a contemptible old age obscure.
   Here rather let me drudge and earn my bread,
   Till vermin or the draff of servile food
   Consume me, and oft-invocated death
   Hasten the welcome end of all my pains.

Manoa. Wilt thou then serve the *Philistines* with that gift
   Which was expressly giv'n thee to annoy them?
   Better at home lie bed-rid, not only idle,
   Inglorious, unemploy'd, with age out-worn.   580
   But God who caused a fountain at thy prayer
   From the dry ground to spring, thy thirst to allay
   After the brunt of battle, can as easy
   Cause light again within thy eyes to spring,
   Wherewith to serve him better than thou hast;

560 *What boots it*: what does it help.   568 *redundant*: waving, flowing
(the Latin sense).   569 *Robustious*: vigorous (Latin, *robustus*).   571
craze: weaken or break.   574 *draff*: refuse grains from brewing; hence,
any kind of refuse.   *servile food*: food fit for slaves.   578 *to annoy them*:
to harm them.

And I persuade me so; why else this strength
Miraculous yet remaining in those locks?
His might continues in thee not for naught,
Nor shall his wondrous gifts be frustrate thus.

Samson. All otherwise to me my thoughts portend,   590
   That these dark orbs no more shall treat with light,
   Nor th' other light of life continue long,
   But yield to double darkness nigh at hand:
   So much I feel my genial spirits droop,
   My hopes all flat, nature within me seems
   In all her functions weary of herself;
   My race of glory run, and race of shame,
   And I shall shortly be with them that rest.

Manoa. Believe not these suggestions which proceed
   From anguish of the mind and humours black,   600
   That mingle with thy fancy. I however
   Must not omit a Father's timely care
   To prosecute the means of thy deliverance
   By ransom or how else: meanwhile be calm,
   And healing words from these thy friends admit.

Samson. O that torment should not be confined
   To the body's wounds and sores
   With maladies innumerable
   In head, heart, breast, and reins;
   But must secret passage find   610
   To th' inmost mind,
   There exercise all his fierce accidents,
   And on her purest spirits prey,

586 *And I persuade me so*: and I am convinced it is so.   589 *frustrate*:
frustrated.   591 *treat with*: have to do with.   594 *genial spirits*:
vital powers.   600 *humours black*: melancholy moods.   609 *reins*:
kidneys or loins.

As on entrails, joints, and limbs,
With answerable pains, but more intense,
Though void of corporal sense.
  My griefs not only pain me
As a ling'ring disease,
But finding no redress, ferment and rage,
Nor less than wounds immedicable   620
Rankle, and fester, and gangrene,
To black mortification.
Thoughts my Tormentors arm'd with deadly stings
Mangle my apprehensive tenderest parts,
Exasperate, exulcerate, and raise
Dire inflammation which no cooling herb
Or med'cinal liquor can assuage,
Nor breath of Vernal Air from snowy *Alp*.
Sleep hath forsook and giv'n me o'er
To death's benumbing Opium as my only cure.   630
Thence faintings, swoonings of despair,
And sense of Heav'n's desertion.
  I was his nursling once and choice delight,
His destined from the womb,
Promised by Heav'nly message twice descending.
Under his special eye
Abstemious I grew up and thrived amain;
He led me on to mightiest deeds
Above the nerve of mortal arm
Against the uncircumcised, our enemies.   640
But now hath cast me off as never known,
And to those cruel enemies,

615 *answerable*: corresponding.   624 *my apprehensive tenderest parts*:
my mind and imagination.   627 *med'cinal*: medicinal.   635
message: messenger.   637 *Abstemious*: abstaining from wine (the Latin
sense).   *amain*: vigorously.   639 *nerve*: sinew (the Latin sense).

Whom I by his appointment had provoked,
Left me all helpless with th' irreparable loss
Of sight, reserved alive to be repeated
The subject of their cruelty or scorn.
Nor am I in the list of them that hope;
Hopeless are all my evils, all remediless;
This one prayer yet remains, might I be heard,
No long petition, speedy death,   650
The close of all my miseries, and the balm.

Chorus. Many are the sayings of the wise
 In ancient and in modern books enroll'd;
 Extolling Patience as the truest fortitude;
 And to the bearing well of all calamities,
 All chances incident to man's frail life
 Consolatories writ
 With studied argument, and much persuasion sought
 Lenient of grief and anxious thought;
 But with th' afflicted in his pangs their sound   660
 Little prevails, or rather seems a tune
 Harsh, and of dissonant mood from his complaint,
 Unless he feel within
 Some source of consolation from above:
 Secret refreshings, that repair his strength,
 And fainting spirits uphold.
  God of our Fathers, what is man!
 That thou towards him with hand so various,
 Or might I say contrarious,
 Temper'st thy providence through his short course, 670

643 *appointment*: direction or design.   645 *repeated*: made again and
again.   648 *remediless*: irreparable. Accent 'rémediless'.   657-8
'Consoling discourses (*Consolatories*) are written with studied arguments,
and much persuasion is sought' (verbs supplied from 652).   659 *Lenient*:
soothing, relaxing (the Latin sense).   670 *Temper'st*: regulate, control.

Not evenly, as thou rul'st
The Angelic orders and inferior creatures mute,
Irrational and brute.
Nor do I name of men the common rout,
That wand'ring loose about
Grow up and perish, as the summer fly,
Heads without name no more remember'd,
But such as thou hast solemnly elected,
With gifts and graces eminently adorn'd
To some great work, thy glory,   680
And people's safety, which in part they effect:
Yet toward these thus dignified, thou oft
Amidst their highth of noon,
Changest thy countenance, and thy hand with no regard
Of highest favours past
From thee on them, or them to thee of service.
  Nor only dost degrade them, or remit
To life obscured, which were a fair dismission,
But throw'st them lower than thou didst exalt them high,
Unseemly falls in human eye,   690
Too grievous for the trespass or omission;
Oft leav'st them to the hostile sword
Of Heathen and profane, their carcases
To dogs and fowls a prey, or else captived:
Or to the unjust tribunals, under change of times,
And condemnation of the ingrateful multitude.
If these they 'scape, perhaps in poverty
With sickness and disease thou bow'st them down,

674 *rout*: crowd.   677 *Heads without name*: counted by heads without
regard to individuality.   682 *dignified*: raised to positions of dignity.
687 *degrade*: put down from a high position.   *remit*: send back.   688
obscured: hidden from public view.   694 *captived*: accent 'captíved'
(as in 33).

Painful diseases and deform'd,
In crude old age;   700
Though not disordinate, yet causeless suff'ring
The punishment of dissolute days: in fine,
Just or unjust, alike seem miserable,
For oft alike, both come to evil end.
  So deal not with this once thy glorious Champion,
The Image of thy strength, and mighty minister.
What do I beg? how hast thou dealt already?
Behold him in this state calamitous, and turn
His labours, for thou canst, to peaceful end.
  But who is this, what thing of Sea or Land?   710
Female of sex it seems,
That so bedeck'd, ornate and gay,
Comes this way sailing
Like a stately Ship
Of *Tarsus*, bound for th' Isles
Of *Javan* or *Gadier*
With all her bravery on, and tackle trim,
Sails fill'd, and streamers waving,
Courted by all the winds that hold them play.
An Amber scent of odorous perfume   720
Her harbinger, a damsel train behind,
Some rich *Philistian* Matron she may seem;
And now at nearer view, no other certain
Than *Dalila* thy wife.

Samson. My Wife, my Traitress, let her not come near me.

700 *crude*: premature (from the Latin sense, lit. 'unripe').   701
Though not disordinate: though they have not been disordinate, i.e. dissolute.
702 *in fine*: in conclusion, to sum up.   706 *minister*: servant or agent.
717 *bravery*: finery.   *tackle trim*: rigging in good order.   719 *hold*
them play: play or dally with them.   720 *Amber scent*: perfume of grey
amber or ambergris.

Chorus. Yet on she moves, now stands and eyes thee fix'd,
  About t' have spoke, but now, with head declined
  Like a fair flower surcharged with dew, she weeps
  And words address'd seem into tears dissolved,
  Wetting the borders of her silken veil: 730
  But now again she makes address to speak.

Dalila. With doubtful feet and wavering resolution
  I came, still dreading thy displeasure, *Samson*,
  Which to have merited, without excuse,
  I cannot but acknowledge; yet if tears
  May expiate (though the fact more evil drew
  In the perverse event than I foresaw)
  My penance hath not slacken'd, though my pardon
  No way assured. But conjugal affection
  Prevailing over fear, and timorous doubt   740
  Hath led me on desirous to behold
  Once more thy face, and know of thy estate,
  If aught in my ability may serve
  To lighten what thou suffer'st, and appease.
  Thy mind with what amends is in my power,
  Though late, yet in some part to recompense
  My rash but more unfortunate misdeed.

Samson. Out, out *Hyaena*; these are thy wonted arts,
  And arts of every woman false like thee,
  To break all faith, all vows, deceive, betray,   750
  Then as repentant to submit, beseech,

727 *declined*: bent down.   728 *surcharged*: over-burdened.   729
address'd: prepared or proffered (see also 731).   734–5 'I cannot but
admit that I have deserved this displeasure of yours, and I have nothing to
say in excuse.'   736 *fact*: action.   *more evil drew*: had more evil
consequences.   737 *perverse event*: unexpected result.   738 *penance*:
penitence.   738–9 'although I cannot be at all sure of obtaining
pardon'.   742 *estate*: condition.

And reconcilement move with feign'd remorse,
Confess, and promise wonders in her change:
Not truly penitent, but chief to try
Her husband, how far urged his patience bears,
His virtue or weakness which way to assail.
Then with more cautious and instructed skill
Again transgresses, and again submits;
That wisest and best men full oft beguiled
With goodness principled not to reject   760
The penitent, but ever to forgive,
Are drawn to wear out miserable days,
Entangled with a pois'nous bosom snake,
If not by quick destruction soon cut off
As I by thee, to Ages an example.

Dalila. Yet hear me *Samson*; not that I endeavour
To lessen or extenuate my offence,
But that on th' other side if it be weigh'd
By itself, with aggravations not surcharged,
Or else with just allowance counterpoised,   770
I may, if possible, thy pardon find
The easier towards me, or thy hatred less.
First granting, as I do, it was a weakness
In me, but incident to all our sex,
Curiosity, inquisitive, importune
Of secrets, then with like infirmity
To publish them, both common female faults:
Was it not weakness also to make known

752 *move*: beg.   754 *chief*: chiefly.   754–6 'to test her husband
and find out how long his patience will bear provocation, and in what
way she may attack his goodness or his weakness'.   757 *instructed*:
experienced or better-informed.   760 *With goodness principled not to
reject*: instructed by goodness in the principle that one should not reject.
774 *incident to*: occurring in.   775 *importune*: importunate, persistent
in some request.   777 *publish*: reveal.

For importunity, that is for naught,
Wherein consisted all thy strength and safety?   780
To what I did thou show'dst me first the way.
But I to enemies reveal'd, and should not:
Nor shouldst thou have trusted that to woman's frailty;
Ere I to thee, thou to thyself wast cruel.
Let weakness then with weakness come to parle
So near related, or the same of kind,
Thine forgive mine; that men may censure thine
The gentler, if severely thou exact not
More strength from me, than in thyself was found.
And what if Love, which thou interpret'st hate,   790
The jealousy of Love, powerful of sway
In human hearts, nor less in mine towards thee,
Caused what I did? I saw thee mutable
Of fancy, fear'd lest one day thou wouldst leave me
As her at *Timna*, sought by all means therefore
How to endear, and hold thee to me firmest:
No better way I saw than by importuning
To learn thy secrets, get into my power
Thy key of strength and safety. Thou wilt say,
Why then reveal'd? I was assured by those   800
Who tempted me, that nothing was design'd
Against thee but safe custody, and hold:
That made for me, I knew that liberty
Would draw thee forth to perilous enterprises,
While I at home sat full of cares and fears
Wailing thy absence in my widow'd bed;
Here I should still enjoy thee night and day
Mine and Love's pris'ner, not the *Philistines*',

782 *But I . . . reveal'd*: but, you say, I . . . revealed.   785 *parle*: treaty
or negotiation.   794 *fancy*: affection.   803 *That made for me*: that
was in my favour.

Whole to myself, unhazarded abroad,
Fearless at home of partners in my love.   810
These reasons in Love's law have past for good,
Though fond and reasonless to some perhaps:
And Love hath oft, well meaning, wrought much woe,
Yet always pity or pardon hath obtain'd.
Be not unlike all others, not austere
As thou art strong, inflexible as steel.
If thou in strength all mortals dost exceed,
In uncompassionate anger do not so.

Samson. How cunningly the sorceress displays
    Her own transgressions, to upbraid me mine!   820
    That malice not repentance brought thee hither,
    By this appears: I gave, thou say'st, th' example,
    I led the way; bitter reproach, but true,
    I to myself was false ere thou to me.
    Such pardon therefore as I give my folly,
    Take to thy wicked deed: which when thou seest
    Impartial, self-severe, inexorable,
    Thou wilt renounce thy seeking, and much rather
    Confess it feign'd. Weakness is thy excuse,
    And I believe it, weakness to resist   830
    Philistian gold: if weakness may excuse,
    What Murderer, what Traitor, Parricide,
    Incestuous, Sacrilegious, but may plead it?
    All wickedness is weakness: that plea therefore
    With God or Man will gain thee no remission.
    But Love constrain'd thee; call it furious rage
    To satisfy thy lust: Love seeks to have Love;

812 *fond*: foolish.   820 *upbraid me mine*: upbraid me with mine.
826-7 'And when you see the "pardon" I give myself to be an impartial,
inexorable, self-condemnation', &c.   836 *But Love constrain'd thee*:
but, you say, Love constrained you.

My love how couldst thou hope, who took'st the way
To raise in me inexpiable hate,
Knowing, as needs I must, by thee betray'd?   840
In vain thou striv'st to cover shame with shame,
Or by evasions thy crime uncover'st more.

Dalila. Since thou determin'st weakness for no plea
 In man or woman, though to thy own condemning,
 Hear what assaults I had, what snares besides,
 What sieges girt me round, ere I consented;
 Which might have awed the best-resolved of men,
 The constantest, to have yielded without blame.
 It was not gold, as to my charge thou lay'st,
 That wrought with me: thou know'st the Magistrates 850
 And Princes of my country came in person,
 Solicited, commanded, threaten'd, urged,
 Adjured by all the bonds of civil Duty
 And of Religion, press'd how just it was,
 How honourable, how glorious to entrap
 A common enemy, who had destroy'd
 Such numbers of our Nation: and the Priest
 Was not behind, but ever at my ear,
 Preaching how meritorious with the gods
 It would be to ensnare an irreligious   860
 Dishonourer of *Dagon*. What had I
 To oppose against such powerful arguments?
 Only my love of thee held long debate,
 And combated in silence all these reasons
 With hard contest. At length that grounded maxim
 So rife and celebrated in the mouths

840 'knowing myself . . . to be betrayed by thee'.   847 *awed*:
impressed.   854 *press'd*: emphasized.   865 *grounded*: firmly
established.   866 *rife*: widespread or common.   *celebrated*: often
repeated (the Latin sense).

Of wisest men, that to the public good
Private respects must yield, with grave authority
Took full possession of me and prevail'd;
Virtue, as I thought, truth, duty so enjoining.   870

Samson. I thought where all thy circling wiles would end:
In feign'd Religion, smooth hypocrisy.
But had thy love, still odiously pretended,
Been, as it ought, sincere, it would have taught thee
Far other reasonings, brought forth other deeds.
I before all the daughters of my Tribe
And of my Nation, chose thee from among
My enemies, loved thee, as too well thou knew'st,
Too well, unbosom'd all my secrets to thee,
Not out of levity, but over-power'd   880
By thy request, who could deny thee nothing;
Yet now am judged an enemy. Why then
Didst thou at first receive me for thy husband?
Then, as since then, thy country's foe profess'd:
Being once a wife, for me thou wast to leave
Parents and country; nor was I their subject,
Nor under their protection but my own,
Thou mine, not theirs. If aught against my life
Thy country sought of thee, it sought unjustly,
Against the law of nature, law of nations,   890
No more thy country, but an impious crew
Of men conspiring to uphold their state
By worse than hostile deeds, violating the ends
For which our country is a name so dear;
Not therefore to be obey'd. But zeal moved thee;

868 *Private respects*: personal considerations.   871 *circling*: indirect, evasive.   884 *thy country's foe profess'd*: an avowed enemy of thy country.   895 *But zeal moved thee*: but, you say, religious fervour urged you on.

To please thy gods thou didst it; gods unable
To acquit themselves and prosecute their foes
But by ungodly deeds, the contradiction
Of their own deity, Gods cannot be:
Less therefore to be pleased, obey'd, or fear'd.   900
These false pretexts and varnish'd colours failing,
Bare in thy guilt how foul must thou appear?

Dalila. In argument with men a woman ever
Goes by the worse, whatever be her cause.

Samson. For want of words no doubt, or lack of breath;
Witness when I was worried with thy peals.

Dalila. I was a fool, too rash, and quite mistaken
In what I thought would have succeeded best.
Let me obtain forgiveness of thee, *Samson,*
Afford me place to show what recompense   910
Towards thee I intend for what I have misdone,
Misguided. Only what remains past cure
Bear not too sensibly, nor still insist
To afflict thyself in vain: though sight be lost,
Life yet hath many solaces, enjoy'd
Where other senses want not their delights
At home in leisure and domestic ease,
Exempt from many a care and chance to which
Eye-sight exposes daily men abroad.
I to the Lords will intercede, not doubting   920
Their favourable ear, that I may fetch thee

897 *To acquit themselves:* to discharge their duties or functions as gods;
perhaps, to avenge themselves.   901 *varnish'd colours:* colours laid on
superficially like varnish.   906 *peals:* noisy cries.   913 *too sensibly:*
with too much feeling, or sensibility.   *insist:* persist.   916 *want not:*
lack not.   920-1 *not doubting . . . ear:* not being in any doubt that
they will receive my request favourably.

From forth this loathsome prison-house, to abide
With me, where my redoubled love and care
With nursing diligence, to me glad office,
May ever tend about thee to old age
With all things grateful cheer'd, and so supplied,
That what by me thou hast lost thou least shalt miss.

Samson. No, no, of my condition take no care;
  It fits not; thou and I long since are twain;
  Nor think me so unwary or accursed   930
  To bring my feet once more into the snare
  Where once I have been caught. I know thy trains
  Though dearly to my cost, thy gins, and toils;
  Thy fair enchanted cup, and warbling charms
  No more on me have power, their force is null'd:
  So much of Adder's wisdom I have learnt
  To fence my ear against thy sorceries.
  If in my flower of youth and strength, when all men
  Loved, honour'd, fear'd me, thou alone could hate me
  Thy Husband, slight me, sell me, and forgo me;   940
  How wouldst thou use me now, blind, and thereby
  Deceivable, in most things as a child
  Helpless, thence easily contemn'd, and scorn'd,
  And last neglected? How wouldst thou insult
  When I must live uxorious to thy will
  In perfet thraldom, how again betray me,
  Bearing my words and doings to the Lords

923 *redoubled*: made twice as great.   924 *office*: function, task.
925 *tend about thee*: wait upon you.   926 *grateful*: pleasing (Latin,
gratus).   929 *It fits not*: it is not fitting.   932 *trains*: wiles.
933 *gins*: traps or snares.   *toils*: nets for catching animals.   935
null'd: annulled, cancelled.   944 *insult*: exult, triumph.   945
uxorious: dotingly or submissively fond of a wife (Latin, *uxor*).   946
perfet: perfect.

To gloss upon, and censuring, frown or smile?
This Gaol I count the house of Liberty
To thine, whose doors my feet shall never enter.   950

Dalila. Let me approach at least, and touch thy hand.

Samson. Not for thy life, lest fierce remembrance wake
My sudden rage to tear thee joint by joint.
At distance I forgive thee, go with that;
Bewail thy falsehood, and the pious works
It hath brought forth to make thee memorable
Among illustrious women, faithful wives:
Cherish thy hasten'd widowhood with the gold
Of Matrimonial treason: so farewell.

Dalila. I see thou art implacable, more deaf   960
To prayers, than winds and seas, yet winds to seas
Are reconciled at length, and Sea to Shore:
Thy anger, unappeasable, still rages,
Eternal tempest never to be calm'd.
Why do I humble thus myself, and suing
For peace, reap nothing but repulse and hate?
Bid go with evil omen and the brand
Of infamy upon my name denounced?
To mix with thy concernments I desist
Henceforth, nor too much disapprove my own.   970
Fame if not double-faced is double-mouth'd,
And with contrary blast proclaims most deeds;
On both his wings, one black, the other white,
Bears greatest names in his wild aery flight.
My name perhaps among the Circumcised

948 *gloss upon*: comment on.   *censuring*: judging.   950 *To thine*:
compared to thine.   954 *go with that*: be satisfied with that, and go.
969 *concernments*: affairs.   972 *contrary*: accent 'contráry'.   975
the Circumcised: the Israelites.

In *Dan*, in *Judah*, and the bordering tribes,
To all posterity may stand defamed,
With malediction mention'd, and the blot
Of falsehood most unconjugal traduced.
But in my country where I most desire,   980
In *Ecron*, *Gaza*, *Asdod*, and in *Gath*
I shall be named among the famousest
Of Women, sung at solemn festivals,
Living and dead recorded, who to save
Her country from a fierce destroyer, chose
Above the faith of wedlock-bands; my tomb
With odours visited and annual flowers:
Not less renown'd than in Mount *Ephraim*,
Jael, who with inhospitable guile
'Smote *Sisera* sleeping through the Temples nail'd.   990
Nor shall I count it heinous to enjoy
The public marks of honour and reward
Conferr'd upon me, for the piety
Which to my country I was judged to have shown.
At this whoever envies or repines
I leave him to his lot, and like my own.

Chorus. She's gone, a manifest Serpent by her sting
    Discover'd in the end, till now conceal'd.

Samson. So let her go; God sent her to debase me,
    And aggravate my folly who committed   1000
    To such a viper his most sacred trust
    Of secrecy, my safety, and my life.

Chorus. Yet beauty, though injurious, hath strange power,
    After offence returning, to regain

984–6 'who chose to save her country . . . in preference to (*above*)
keeping her faith as a wife'.   987 *odours*: incense.   1000 *aggra-
vate*: to make heavier, to increase (the Latin sense).

Love once possess'd, nor can be easily
Repulsed, without much inward passion felt
And secret sting of amorous remorse.

Samson. Love-quarrels oft in pleasing concord end,
 Not wedlock-treachery endangering life.

Chorus. It is not virtue, wisdom, valour, wit,   1010
 Strength, comeliness of shape, or amplest merit
 That woman's love can win or long inherit;
 But what it is, hard is to say,
 Harder to hit,
 (Which way soever men refer it):
 Much like thy riddle, *Samson*, in one day
 Or seven, though one should musing sit.
  If any of these or all, the *Timnian* bride
 Had not so soon preferr'd
 Thy Paranymph, worthless to thee compared,   1020
 Successor in thy bed;
 Nor both so loosely disallied
 Their nuptials, nor this last so treacherously
 Had shorn the fatal harvest of thy head.
 Is it for that such outward ornament
 Was lavish'd on their Sex, that inward gifts
 Were left for haste unfinish'd, judgement scant,
 Capacity not raised to apprehend
 Or value what is best

1006 *passion*: suffering (Latin, *passio*).   1007 *remorse*: regret, sorrow.
1012 *inherit*: possess.   1015 *Which way soever men refer it*: in however
many different ways men may turn the problem about in their minds.
1016–17 *in one day . . . sit*: whether one sat thinking about it for one day
or seven days.   1018 *If any of these or all*: if any or all of the attractions
already mentioned (1010–11) were effective.   1020 *Paranymph*: best
man.   1022 *disallied*: untied.   1025 *for that*: because.   1027
for haste: in haste, owing to lack of time.

In choice, but oftest to affect the wrong?   1030
Or was too much of self-love mix'd,
Of constancy no root infix'd,
That either they love nothing, or not long?
  Whate'er it be, to wisest men and best
Seeming at first all heav'nly under virgin veil,
Soft, modest, meek, demure,
Once join'd, the contrary she proves, a thorn
Intestine, far within defensive arms
A cleaving mischief, in his way to virtue
Adverse and turbulent; or by her charms   1040
Draws him awry enslaved
With dotage, and his sense depraved
To folly and shameful deeds which ruin ends.
What Pilot so expert but needs must wreck
Embark'd with such a Steers-mate at the Helm?
  Favour'd of Heav'n who finds
One virtuous rarely found,
That in domestic good combines:
Happy that house! his way to peace is smooth:
But virtue which breaks through all opposition,   1050
And all temptation can remove,
Most shines and most is acceptable above.
  Therefore God's universal Law
Gave to the man despotic power
Over his female in due awe,
Nor from that right to part an hour,
Smile she or lour;
So shall he least confusion draw

1030 *affect*: have a liking for, prefer.   1037 *Once join'd*: once married.
1038 *Intestine*: internal.   *far within defensive arms*: having penetrated all
defences.   1046 *Favour'd of Heav'n who finds*: He is favoured by God
who finds, &c.   1048 *combines*: i.e. with her husband; acts in agreement with him.   1057 *lour*: frown, look sullen.

On his whole life, not sway'd
By female usurpation, nor dismay'd.   1060
  But had we best retire, I see a storm?

Samson. Fair days have oft contracted wind and rain.

Chorus. But this another kind of tempest brings.

Samson. Be less abstruse, my riddling days are past.

Chorus. Look now for no enchanting voice, nor fear
  The bait of honey'd words; a rougher tongue
  Draws hitherward, I know him by his stride,
  The Giant *Harapha* of *Gath*, his look
  Haughty as is his pile high-built and proud.
  Comes he in peace? what wind hath blown him hither
  I less conjecture than when first I saw   1071
  The sumptuous *Dalila* floating this way:
  His habit carries peace, his brow defiance.

Samson. Or peace or not, alike to me he comes.

Chorus. His fraught we soon shall know, he now arrives.

Harapha. I come not *Samson*, to condole thy chance,
  As these perhaps, yet wish it had not been,
  Though for no friendly intent. I am of *Gath*,
  Men call me *Harapha*, of stock renown'd
  As *Og* or *Anak* and the *Emims* old   1080
  That *Kiriathaim* held: thou know'st me now
  If thou at all art known. Much I have heard
  Of thy prodigious might and feats perform'd

1062 *contracted*: become involved in, incurred.   1069 *his pile high-built*: his gigantic body ('pile' is the Latin *moles*).   1070 *what wind hath blown him hither*: what purpose brings him here.   1073 *His habit carries peace*: he is dressed as for every-day affairs, i.e. not stripped or armed for combat.   1075 *fraught*: freight, i.e. intention.   1077 *As these*: i.e. the Chorus.

Incredible to me, in this displeased,
That I was never present on the place
Of those encounters, where we might have tried
Each other's force in camp or listed field:
And now am come to see of whom such noise
Hath walk'd about, and each limb to survey,
If thy appearance answer loud report.   1090

Samson. The way to know were not to see but taste.

Harapha. Dost thou already single me? I thought
  Gyves and the Mill had tamed thee. O that fortune
  Had brought me to the field where thou art famed
  To have wrought such wonders with an Ass's jaw;
  I should have forced thee soon wish other arms,
  Or left thy carcass where the Ass lay thrown.
  So had the glory of Prowess been recover'd
  To *Palestine*, won by a *Philistine*
  From the unforeskinn'd race, of whom thou bear'st 1100
  The highest name for valiant Acts; that honour
  Certain to have won by mortal duel from thee,
  I lose, prevented by thy eyes put out.

Samson. Boast not of what thou wouldst have done, but do
  What then thou wouldst; thou seest it in thy hand.

Harapha. To combat with a blind man I disdain,
  And thou hast need much washing to be touch'd.

Samson. Such usage as your honourable Lords
  Afford me assassinated and betray'd,

1087 *camp*: field of combat (Italian, *campo*).   *listed*: roped off with
'lists', i.e. strips of cloth, as for a tournament.   1088 *noise*: rumour,
report.   1091 *taste*: try by personal experience.   1092 *single*:
pick out, challenge to single combat.   1093 *Gyves*: ankle-fetters.
1100 *unforeskinn'd*: circumcised.   1102 *mortal duel*: duel to the death.
1105 *in thy hand*: offered to thee.   1109 *assassinated*: attacked by treachery.

Who durst not with their whole united powers   1110
In fight withstand me single and unarm'd,
Nor in the house with chamber Ambushes
Close-banded durst attack me, no, not sleeping,
Till they had hired a woman with their gold
Breaking her Marriage Faith to circumvent me.
Therefore without feign'd shifts let be assign'd
Some narrow place enclosed, where sight may give thee,
Or rather flight, no great advantage on me;
Then put on all thy gorgeous arms, thy Helmet
And Brigandine of brass, thy broad Habergeon,   1120
Vant-brass and Greaves, and Gauntlet, add thy Spear
A Weaver's beam, and seven-times-folded shield;
I only with an Oaken staff will meet thee,
And raise such outcries on thy clatter'd Iron,
Which long shall not withhold me from thy head,
That in a little time while breath remains thee,
Thou oft shalt wish thyself at *Gath* to boast
Again in safety what thou wouldst have done
To *Samson*, but shalt never see *Gath* more.

Harapha. Thou durst not thus disparage glorious arms
  Which greatest Heroes have in battle worn,   1131
  Their ornament and safety, had not spells
  And black enchantments, some Magician's Art
  Arm'd thee or charm'd thee strong, which thou from
      Heaven
  Feign'dst at thy birth was giv'n thee in thy hair,

1112 *chamber Ambushes*: surprise attacks indoors.   1113 *Close-banded*: banded together secretly.   1116 *shifts*: tricks, evasions; here excuses.   1120 *Brigandine*: armoured tunic.   *Habergeon*: chain-mail or plate covering neck and shoulders.   1121 *Vant-brass*: armour for the fore-arm (French, *avant-bras*).   *Greaves*: leg-armour.   *Gauntlet*: glove of mail (French, *gant*).

Where strength can least abide, though all thy hairs
Were bristles ranged like those that ridge the back
Of chafed wild Boars, or ruffled Porcupines.

Samson. I know no Spells, use no forbidden Arts;
My trust is in the living God who gave me   1140
At my Nativity this strength, diffused
No less through all my sinews, joints and bones,
Than thine, while I preserved these locks unshorn,
The pledge of my unviolated vow.
For proof hereof, if *Dagon* be thy god,
Go to his Temple, invocate his aid
With solemnest devotion, spread before him
How highly it concerns his glory now
To frustrate and dissolve these Magic spells,
Which I to be the power of *Israel*'s God   1150
Avow, and challenge *Dagon* to the test,
Offering to combat thee his Champion bold,
With th' utmost of his Godhead seconded:
Then thou shalt see, or rather to thy sorrow
Soon feel, whose God is strongest, thine or mine.

Harapha. Presume not on thy God, whate'er he be,
Thee he regards not, owns not, hath cut off
Quite from his people, and deliver'd up
Into thy Enemies' hand, permitted them
To put out both thine eyes, and fetter'd send thee   1160
Into the common Prison, there to grind
Among the Slaves and Asses thy comrades,
As good for nothing else; no better service
With those thy boist'rous locks, no worthy match

1138 *chafed*: angered (French, *chauffer*).   1143 *while I preserved*: for
as long as I should preserve.   1147 *spread before him*: explain to him.
1162 *comrades*: accent 'comrádes'.   1164 *boist'rous*: vigorous, flourishing.

For valour to assail, nor by the sword
Of noble Warrior, so to stain his honour,
But by the Barber's razor best subdued.

Samson. All these indignities, for such they are
From thine, these evils I deserve and more,
Acknowledge them from God inflicted on me   1170
Justly, yet despair not of his final pardon
Whose ear is ever open, and his eye
Gracious to re-admit the suppliant;
In confidence whereof I once again
Defy thee to the trial of mortal fight,
By combat to decide whose god is God,
Thine or whom I with *Israel*'s Sons adore.

Harapha. Fair honour that thou dost thy God, in trusting
He will accept thee to defend his cause,
A Murderer, a Revolter, and a Robber.   1180

Samson. Tongue-doughty Giant, how dost thou prove me
    these?

Harapha. Is not thy Nation subject to our Lords?
Their Magistrates confess'd it, when they took thee
As a League-breaker and deliver'd bound
Into our hands: for hadst thou not committed
Notorious murder on those thirty men
At *Askalon*, who never did thee harm,
Then like a Robber stripp'dst them of their robes?
The *Philistines*, when thou hadst broke the league,
Went up with armed powers thee only seeking,   1190
To others did no violence nor spoil.

1168 *indignities*: humiliations.   1175 *Defy*: challenge.   1180
Revolter: rebel.   1181 *Tongue-doughty*: valiant in words only.
1184 *League-breaker*: treaty-breaker.

Samson. Among the Daughters of the *Philistines*
I chose a Wife, which argued me no foe;
And in your City held my Nuptial Feast:
But your ill-meaning Politician Lords,
Under pretence of Bridal friends and guests,
Appointed to await me thirty spies,
Who threat'ning cruel death constrain'd the bride
To wring from me and tell to them my secret,
That solved the riddle which I had proposed.   1200
When I perceived all set on enmity,
As on my enemies, wherever chanced,
I used hostility, and took their spoil
To pay my underminers in their coin.
My Nation was subjected to your Lords:
It was the force of Conquest; force with force
Is well ejected when the Conquer'd can.
But I a private person, whom my Country
As a league-breaker gave up bound, presumed
Single Rebellion and did Hostile Acts: 1210
I was no private but a person raised
With strength sufficient and command from Heav'n
To free my Country; if their servile minds
Me their Deliverer sent would not receive,
But to their Masters gave me up for naught,
Th' unworthier they; whence to this day they serve.
I was to do my part from Heav'n assign'd,
And had perform'd it if my known offence
Had not disabled me, not all your force.
These shifts refuted, answer thy appellant   1220

1195 *Politician*: intriguing for power.   1204 *my underminers*: those who
attacked me secretly or insidiously.   1208 *But I a private person*:
but, you say, I, though only a private person, &c.   1217 *I was to do*: it
was for me to do.   1220 *appellant*: the challenger to a combat (as
'calling out' the defendant).

Though by his blindness maim'd for high attempts,
Who now defies thee thrice to single fight,
As a petty enterprise of small enforce.

Harapha. With thee a Man condemn'd, a Slave enroll'd,
Due by the Law to capital punishment?
To fight with thee no man of arms will deign.

Samson. Cam'st thou for this, vain boaster, to survey me,
To descant on my strength, and give thy verdit?
Come nearer, part not hence so slight inform'd;
But take good heed my hand survey not thee.   1230

Harapha. O *Baal-zebub*! can my ears unused
Hear these dishonours, and not render death?

Samson. No man withholds thee, nothing from thy hand
Fear I incurable; bring up thy van,
My heels are fetter'd, but my fist is free.

Harapha. This insolence other kind of answer fits.

Samson. Go baffled coward, lest I run upon thee,
Though in these chains, bulk without spirit vast,
And with one buffet lay thy structure low,
Or swing thee in the Air, then dash thee down   1240
To the hazard of thy brains and shatter'd sides.

Harapha. By *Astaroth* ere long thou shalt lament
These braveries in Irons loaden on thee.

Chorus. His Giantship is gone somewhat crestfall'n,
Stalking with less unconsci'nable strides,
And lower looks, but in a sultry chafe.

1223 *of small enforce*: easy to make good.   1228 *descant*: comment at
length.   1234 *van*: vanguard.   1238 *bulk without spirit vast*: vast
bulk without courage or energy.   1243 *braveries*: acts or words
of defiance.   1244 *crestfall'n*: cast down in spirits.   1245 *unconsci'nable*: i.e. unconscionable, unreasonable or excessive.   1246
chafe: heat of mind or temper.

Samson. I dread him not, nor all his Giant-brood,
 Though Fame divulge him Father of five Sons
 All of Gigantic size, *Goliah* chief.

Chorus. He will directly to the Lords, I fear,   1250
 And with malicious counsel stir them up
 Some way or other yet further to afflict thee.

Samson. He must allege some cause, and offer'd fight
 Will not dare mention, lest a question rise
 Whether he durst accept the offer or not,
 And that he durst not plain enough appear'd.
 Much more affliction than already felt
 They cannot well impose, nor I sustain,
 If they intend advantage of my labours,
 The work of many hands, which earns my keeping   1260
 With no small profit daily to my owners.
 But come what will, my deadliest foe will prove
 My speediest friend, by death to rid me hence,
 The worst that he can give, to me the best.
 Yet so it may fall out, because their end
 Is hate, not help to me, it may with mine
 Draw their own ruin who attempt the deed.

Chorus. Oh how comely it is and how reviving
 To the Spirits of just men long oppress'd!
 When God into the hands of their deliverer   1270
 Puts invincible might
 To quell the mighty of the Earth, th' oppressor,
 The brute and boist'rous force of violent men
 Hardy and industrious to support
 Tyrannic power, but raging to pursue
 The righteous and all such as honour Truth;

1248 *divulge him*: proclaim him to be.   1250 *He will directly to the Lords*: 'go' is understood.   1253 *offer'd fight*: my offer to fight him.

He all their Ammunition
And feats of War defeats
With plain Heroic magnitude of mind
And celestial vigour arm'd,   1280
Their Armouries and Magazines contemns,
Renders them useless, while
With winged expedition
Swift as the lightning glance he executes
His errand on the wicked, who surprised
Lose their defence distracted and amazed.
  But Patience is more oft the exercise
Of Saints, the trial of their fortitude,
Making them each his own Deliverer,
And Victor over all   1290
That tyranny or fortune can inflict:
Either of these is in thy lot,
Samson, with might endued
Above the Sons of men; but sight bereaved
May chance to number thee with those
Whom Patience finally must crown.
This Idol's day hath been to thee no day of rest,
  Labouring thy mind
More than the working day thy hands,
And yet perhaps more trouble is behind.   1300
For I descry this way
Some other tending, in his hand
A Sceptre or quaint staff he bears,
Comes on amain, speed in his look.

1277 *Ammunition*: weapons of war.   1281 *Magazines*: stores of arms
or ammunition.   1283 *expedition*: speed.   1294 *sight bereaved*: loss
of sight.   1298 *Labouring thy mind*: causing thy mind to labour.
1300 *behind*: yet to come.   1302 *some other tending*: someone else
approaching.   1303 *quaint*: skilfully or ornamentally worked.
1304 *amain*: at full speed.

By his habit I discern him now
A Public Officer, and now at hand.
His message will be short and voluble.

Officer. *Ebrews*, the Pris'ner *Samson* here I seek.

Chorus. His manacles remark him, there he sits.

Officer. *Samson*, to thee our Lords thus bid me say: 1310
  This day to *Dagon* is a solemn Feast,
  With Sacrifices, Triumph, Pomp, and Games;
  Thy strength they know surpassing human rate,
  And now some public proof thereof require
  To honour this great Feast and great Assembly;
  Rise therefore with all speed and come along,
  Where I will see thee hearten'd and fresh clad
  To appear as fits before th' illustrious Lords.

Samson. Thou know'st I am an *Ebrew*, therefore tell them,
  Our Law forbids at their Religious Rites   1320
  My presence; for that cause I cannot come.

Officer. This answer, be assured, will not content them.

Samson. Have they not Sword-players, and ev'ry sort
  Of Gymnic Artists, Wrestlers, Riders, Runners,
  Jugglers and Dancers, Antics, Mummers, Mimics,
  But they must pick me out with shackles tired,
  And over-labour'd at their public Mill,
  To make them sport with blind activity?
  Do they not seek occasion of new quarrels

1307 *voluble*: rapid in utterance.   1309 *manacles*: here ankle-fetters.
remark: distinguish.   1312 *Triumph*: public procession and festival in
honour of a victory.   1313 *rate*: measure or calculation.   1317
hearten'd: refreshed, strengthened with food or drink.   1324 *Gymnic*:
gymnastic.   1325 *Antics*: grotesquely dressed players or masquers.
Mummers: actors richly or gaudily dressed.

On my refusal to distress me more,   1330
Or make a game of my calamities?
Return the way thou cam'st, I will not come.

Officer. Regard thyself, this will offend them highly.

Samson. Myself? my conscience and internal peace.
Can they think me so broken, so debased
With corporal servitude, that my mind ever
Will condescend to such absurd commands?
Although their drudge, to be their fool or jester,
And in my midst of sorrow and heart-grief
To show them feats, and play before their god,   1340
The worst of all indignities, yet on me
Join'd with extreme contempt? I will not come.

Officer. My message was imposed on me with speed,
Brooks no delay; is this thy resolution?

Samson. So take it with what speed thy message needs.

Officer. I am sorry what this stoutness will produce.

Samson. Perhaps thou shalt have cause to sorrow indeed.

Chorus. Consider, *Samson*; matters now are strain'd
Up to the highth, whether to hold or break;
He's gone, and who knows how he may report   1350
Thy words by adding fuel to the flame?
Expect another message more imperious,
More Lordly thund'ring than thou well wilt bear.

Samson. Shall I abuse this Consecrated gift

1333 *Regard thyself*: consider your own interests.   1334 *internal*:
mental or spiritual.   1342 *Join'd*: enjoined, commanded.   1344
Brooks: bears, puts up with.   1346 *I am sorry what*: I am sorry to
think what.   *stoutness*: courage, especially of a proud, assertive kind;
stubbornness or arrogance.

Of strength, again returning with my hair
After my great transgression, so requite
Favour renew'd, and add a greater sin
By prostituting holy things to Idols;
A Nazarite in place abominable
Vaunting my strength in honour to their *Dagon*?   1360
Besides, how vile, contemptible, ridiculous,
What act more execrably unclean, profane?

Chorus. Yet with this strength thou serv'st the *Philistines*,
Idolatrous, uncircumcised, unclean.

Samson. Not in their Idol-worship, but by labour
Honest and lawful to deserve my food
Of those who have me in their civil power.

Chorus. Where the heart joins not, outward acts defile not.

Samson. Where outward force constrains, the sentence
   holds;
But who constrains me to the Temple of *Dagon*,   1370
Not dragging? The Philistian Lords command:
Commands are no constraints. If I obey them,
I do it freely; venturing to displease
God for the fear of Man, and Man prefer,
Set God behind: which in his jealousy
Shall never, unrepented, find forgiveness.
Yet that he may dispense with me or thee
Present in Temples at Idolatrous Rites
For some important cause, thou need'st not doubt.

1360 *Vaunting*: displaying proudly.   1362 *unclean*: i.e. not permitted by the Mosaic law.   1367 *civil*: political (Latin, *civilis*).   1369
the sentence holds: the maxim holds good or applies.   1375 *which*: an
action which.   1376 *unrepented*: if not repented of.   1377–8 'that
he may grant thee or me a special dispensation enabling us to be present
at idolatrous rites'.

Chorus. How thou wilt here come off surmounts my reach.

Samson. Be of good courage, I begin to feel   1381
  Some rousing motions in me which dispose
  To something extraordinary my thoughts.
  I with this Messenger will go along,
  Nothing to do, be sure, that may dishonour
  Our Law, or stain my vow of *Nazarite*.
  If there be aught of presage in the mind,
  This day will be remarkable in my life
  By some great act, or of my days the last.

Chorus. In time thou hast resolved, the man returns.   1390

Officer. Samson, this second message from our Lords
  To thee I am bid say. Art thou our Slave,
  Our Captive, at the public Mill our drudge,
  And dar'st thou at our sending and command
  Dispute thy coming? come without delay;
  Or we shall find such Engines to assail
  And hamper thee, as thou shalt come of force,
  Though thou wert firmlier fasten'd than a rock.

Samson. I could be well content to try their Art,
  Which to no few of them would prove pernicious.   1400
  Yet knowing their advantages too many,
  Because they shall not trail me through their streets
  Like a wild Beast, I am content to go.
  Masters' commands come with a power resistless
  To such as owe them absolute subjection;
  And for a life who will not change his purpose?
  (So mutable are all the ways of men!)

1380 *come off*: extricate yourself from danger.   *surmounts my reach*: is beyond my understanding or imagination.   1396 *Engines*: means or devices.   1397 *hamper*: bind or constrain.   *of force*: of necessity.
1400 *pernicious*: deadly.   1402 *Because*: in order that.

Yet this be sure, in nothing to comply
Scandalous or forbidden in our Law.

Officer. I praise thy resolution, doff these links: 1410
 By this compliance thou wilt win the Lords
 To favour, and perhaps to set thee free.

Samson. Brethren farewell, your company along
 I will not wish, lest it perhaps offend them
 To see me girt with Friends; and how the sight
 Of me as of a common Enemy,
 So dreaded once, may now exasperate them
 I know not. Lords are Lordliest in their wine;
 And the well-feasted Priest then soonest fired
 With zeal, if aught Religion seem concern'd: 1420
 No less the people on their Holy-days
 Impetuous, insolent, unquenchable.
 Happen what may, of me expect to hear
 Nothing dishonourable, impure, unworthy
 Our God, our Law, my Nation, or myself;
 The last of me or no I cannot warrant.

Chorus. Go, and the Holy One
 Of *Israel* be thy guide
 To what may serve his glory best, and spread his name
 Great among the Heathen round: 1430
 Send thee the Angel of thy Birth, to stand
 Fast by thy side, who from thy Father's field
 Rode up in flames after his message told
 Of thy conception, and be now a shield
 Of fire; that Spirit that first rush'd on thee

1410 *doff*: do off.   1420 *if aught*: if in any way (Latin, *si quid*).
1426 'Whether this will be the last you hear of me or not I cannot be
certain.'   1431 *Send thee*: God send thee.   1433 *after his message
told*: after delivering his message.

In the camp of *Dan*
Be efficacious in thee now at need.
For never was from Heav'n imparted
Measure of strength so great to mortal seed,
As in thy wondrous actions hath been seen.   1440
But wherefore comes old *Manoa* in such haste
With youthful steps? much livelier than erewhile
He seems: supposing here to find his Son,
Or of him bringing to us some glad news?

Manoa. Peace with you brethren; my inducement hither
Was not at present here to find my Son,
By order of the Lords new parted hence
To come and play before them at their Feast.
I heard all as I came, the City rings
And numbers thither flock; I had no will,   1450
Lest I should see him forced to things unseemly.
But that which moved my coming now, was chiefly
To give ye part with me what hope I have
With good success to work his liberty.

Chorus. That hope would much rejoice us to partake
With thee; say reverend Sire, we thirst to hear.

Manoa. I have attempted one by one the Lords
Either at home, or through the high street passing,
With supplication prone and Father's tears
To accept of ransom for my Son their pris'ner.   1460
Some much averse I found and wondrous harsh,
Contemptuous, proud, set on revenge and spite:
That part most reverenced *Dagon* and his Priests;
Others more moderate seeming, but their aim

1439 *mortal seed*: the human race.   1445 *my inducement hither*: what
has led me here.   1453 *To give ye part with me*: to share with you.
1457 *attempted*: tested by making proposals.

Private reward, for which both God and State
They easily would set to sale; a third
More generous far and civil, who confess'd
They had enough revenged, having reduced
Their foe to misery beneath their fears:
The rest was magnanimity to remit,   1470
If some convenient ransom were proposed.
What noise or shout was that? it tore the sky.

Chorus. Doubtless the people shouting to behold
  Their once great dread, captive, and blind before them,
  Or at some proof of strength before them shown.

Manoa. His ransom, if my whole inheritance
  May compass it, shall willingly be paid
  And number'd down: much rather shall I choose
  To live the poorest in my Tribe than richest,
  And he in that calamitous prison left.   1480
  No, I am fix'd not to part hence without him;
  For his redemption all my Patrimony,
  If need be, I am ready to forgo
  And quit: not wanting him, I shall want nothing.

Chorus. Fathers are wont to lay up for their Sons,
  Thou for thy Son art bent to lay out all;
  Sons wont to nurse their Parents in old age,
  Thou in old age car'st how to nurse thy Son,
  Made older than thy age through eye-sight lost.

Manoa. It shall be my delight to tend his eyes,   1490
  And view him sitting in the house, ennobled

1470 *The rest was magnanimity to remit*: it would be generous to remit the
remaining punishment.   1474 *Their once great dread*: i.e. Samson,
whom formerly they so dreaded.   1481 *fix'd*: resolved.   *part*: go
(French, *partir*).   1484 *wanting*: lacking.   1486 *bent*: eager.

With all those high exploits by him achieved,
And on his shoulders waving down those locks,
That of a Nation arm'd the strength contain'd:
And I persuade me God had not permitted
His strength again to grow up with his hair
Garrison'd round about him like a Camp
Of faithful Soldiery, were not his purpose
To use him further yet in some great service,
Not to sit idle with so great a gift   1500
Useless, and thence ridiculous about him.
And since his strength with eye-sight was not lost,
God will restore him eye-sight to his strength.

Chorus. Thy hopes are not ill-founded nor seem vain
Of his delivery, and thy joy thereon
Conceived, agreeable to a Father's love;
In both which we, as next, participate.

Manoa. I know your friendly minds and—O what noise!
Mercy of Heav'n, what hideous noise was that?
Horribly loud, unlike the former shout.   1510

Chorus. Noise call you it or universal groan
As if the whole inhabitation perish'd,
Blood, death, and deathful deeds are in that noise,
Ruin, destruction at the utmost point.

Manoa. Of ruin indeed methought I heard the noise,
Oh it continues, they have slain my Son.

Chorus. Thy Son is rather slaying them, that outcry
From slaughter of one foe could not ascend.

    1498 *were not his purpose*: if his purpose were not.   1503 *to his strength*: to match his strength.   1506 *agreeable to*: corresponding to. 1507 *as next*: i.e. in kinship.   1512 *inhabitation*: community or inhabitants.   1515 *ruin*: collapse (Latin, *ruina*).

Manoa. Some dismal accident it needs must be;
  What shall we do, stay here or run and see?   1520

Chorus. Best keep together here, lest running thither
  We unawares run into danger's mouth.
  This evil on the *Philistines* is fall'n,
  From whom could else a general cry be heard?
  The sufferers then will scarce molest us here,
  From other hands we need not much to fear.
  What if his eye-sight (for to *Israel*'s God
  Nothing is hard) by miracle restored,
  He now be dealing dole among his foes,
  And among heaps of slaughter'd walk his way?   1530

Manoa. That were a joy presumptuous to be thought.

Chorus. Yet God hath wrought things as incredible
  For his people of old; what hinders now?

Manoa. He can I know, but doubt to think he will;
  Yet Hope would fain subscribe, and tempts Belief.
  A little stay will bring some notice hither.

Chorus. Of good or bad so great, of bad the sooner;
  For evil news rides post, while good news baits.
  And to our wish I see one hither speeding,
  An *Ebrew*, as I guess, and of our Tribe.   1540

Messenger. O whither shall I run, or which way fly
  The sight of this so horrid spectacle
  Which erst my eyes beheld and yet behold;
  For dire imagination still pursues me.
  But providence or instinct of nature seems,

1529 *dole*: *both* a portion *and* pain or grief.
scribe: would willingly support (such an idea).
swiftly.   *baits*: dawdles.   1543 *erst*: lately.
1535 *would fain sub-*
1538 *rides post*: travels

Or reason though disturb'd and scarce consulted,
To have guided me aright, I know not how,
To thee first, reverend *Manoa*, and to these
My Countrymen, whom here I knew remaining,
As at some distance from the place of horror,   1550
So in the sad event too much concern'd.

Manoa. The accident was loud, and here before thee
  With rueful cry, yet what it was we hear not;
  No Preface needs, thou see'st we long to know.

Messenger. It would burst forth, but I recover breath
  And sense distract, to know what well I utter.

Manoa. Tell us the sum, the circumstance defer.

Messenger. Gaza yet stands, but all her Sons are fall'n,
  All in a moment overwhelm'd and fall'n.

Manoa. Sad, but thou know'st to *Israelites* not saddest   1560
  The desolation of a Hostile City.

Messenger. Feed on that first, there may be grief in surfeit.

Manoa. Relate by whom. *Messenger.* By *Samson. Manoa.*
      That still lessens
  The sorrow, and converts it nigh to joy.

Messenger. Ah *Manoa* I refrain, too suddenly
  To utter what will come at last too soon;
  Lest evil tidings with too rude irruption
  Hitting thy aged ear should pierce too deep.

Manoa. Suspense in news is torture, speak them out.

Messenger. Then take the worst in brief, *Samson* is dead.

1554 *No Preface needs*: there is no need for preliminary explanations.
1556 *distract*: distracted.   1557 *the sum*: the total result.   *the circumstance*: the details.   1562 *surfeit*: feeding to excess.

Manoa. The worst indeed, O all my hopes defeated   1571
  To free him hence! but death who sets all free
  Hath paid his ransom now and full discharge.
  What windy joy this day had I conceived
  Hopeful of his Delivery, which now proves
  Abortive as the first-born bloom of spring
  Nipp'd with the lagging rear of winter's frost.
  Yet ere I give the reins to grief, say first,
  How died he? death to life is crown or shame.
  All by him fell thou say'st, by whom fell he,   1580
  What glorious hand gave *Samson* his death's wound?

Messenger. Unwounded of his enemies he fell.

Manoa. Wearied with slaughter then or how? explain.

Messenger. By his own hands. *Manoa*. Self-violence? what
      cause
  Brought him so soon at variance with himself
  Among his foes? *Messenger*. Inevitable cause
  At once both to destroy and be destroy'd;
  The Edifice where all were met to see him
  Upon their heads and on his own he pull'd.

Manoa. O lastly over-strong against thyself!   1590
  A dreadful way thou took'st to thy revenge.
  More than enough we know; but while things yet
  Are in confusion, give us if thou canst,
  Eye-witness of what first or last was done,
  Relation more particular and distinct.

Messenger. Occasions drew me early to this City,
  And as the gates I enter'd with Sun-rise,

1574 *windy joy*: vain or empty joy.   1594 *Eye-witness*: as having
been an eye-witness.   1596 *Occasions*: business matters.

The morning Trumpets Festival proclaim'd
Through each high street: little I had despatch'd
When all abroad was rumour'd that this day   1600
Samson should be brought forth to show the people
Proof of his mighty strength in feats and games;
I sorrow'd at his captive state, but minded
Not to be absent at that spectacle.
The building was a spacious Theatre
Half round on two main Pillars vaulted high,
With seats where all the Lords and each degree
Of sort might sit in order to behold;
The other side was open, where the throng
On banks and scaffolds under Sky might stand: 1610
I among these aloof obscurely stood.
The Feast and noon grew high, and Sacrifice
Had fill'd their hearts with mirth, high cheer, and wine,
When to their sports they turn'd. Immediately
Was *Samson* as a public servant brought,
In their state Livery clad; before him Pipes
And Timbrels, on each side went armed guards,
Both horse and foot before him and behind
Archers, and Slingers, Cataphracts and Spears.
At sight of him the people with a shout   1620
Rifted the Air, clamouring their god with praise,
Who had made their dreadful enemy their thrall.
He patient but undaunted where they led him,
Came to the place, and what was set before him

1599 *high street*: main street.   *little I had despatch'd*: I had done little
of my business.   1603 *minded*: resolved, intended.   1608 *sort*:
quality or distinction.   *in order*: placed according to rank.   1610
banks: benches.   1616 *state Livery*: state uniform.   1617 *Timbrels*:
musical instruments of percussion, perhaps tambourines.   1619 *Cataphracts*: men in armour on horses also in armour.   *Spears*: men armed
with spears.   1621 *Rifted*: split.   *clamouring*: acclaiming.

Which without help of eye, might be assay'd,
To heave, pull, draw, or break, he still perform'd
All with incredible, stupendious force,
None daring to appear Antagonist.
At length for intermission sake they led him
Between the pillars; he his guide requested   1630
(For so from such as nearer stood we heard)
As over-tired to let him lean awhile
With both his arms on those two massy Pillars
That to the arched roof gave main support.
He unsuspicious led him; which when *Samson*
Felt in his arms, with head awhile inclined,
And eyes fast fix'd he stood, as one who pray'd,
Or some great matter in his mind revolved.
At last with head erect thus cried aloud:
Hitherto, Lords, what your commands imposed   1640
I have perform'd, as reason was, obeying,
Not without wonder or delight beheld.
Now of my own accord such other trial
I mean to show you of my strength, yet greater;
As with amaze shall strike all who behold.
This utter'd, straining all his nerves he bow'd;
As with the force of winds and waters pent,
When Mountains tremble, those two massy Pillars
With horrible convulsion to and fro,
He tugg'd, he shook, till down they came and drew   1650
The whole roof after them, with burst of thunder
Upon the heads of all who sat beneath,
Lords, Ladies, Captains, Counsellors, or Priests,
Their choice nobility and flower, not only
Of this but each *Philistian* City round
Met from all parts to solemnize this Feast.

1626 *still*: on each occasion.   1633 *massy*: massive.

Samson with these immix'd, inevitably
Pull'd down the same destruction on himself;
The vulgar only 'scaped who stood without.

Chorus. O dearly-bought revenge, yet glorious!   1660
Living or dying thou hast fulfill'd
The work for which thou wast foretold
To *Israel*, and now ly'st victorious
Among thy slain self-kill'd,
Not willingly, but tangled in the fold
Of dire necessity, whose law in death conjoin'd
Thee with thy slaughter'd foes in number more
Than all thy life had slain before.

Semichorus. While their hearts were jocund and sublime,
Drunk with Idolatry, drunk with Wine,   1670
And fat regorged of Bulls and Goats,
Chaunting their Idol, and preferring
Before our living Dread who dwells
In *Silo* his bright Sanctuary:
Among them he a spirit of frenzy sent,
Who hurt their minds,
And urged them on with mad desire
To call in haste for their destroyer;
They only set on sport and play
Unweetingly importuned   1680
Their own destruction to come speedy upon them.
So fond are mortal men
Fall'n into wrath divine,

1659 *The vulgar*: the common people.   *'scaped*: escaped.   1663
ly'st: liest.   1666 *necessity*: fate.   1669 *sublime*: elated (Latin,
sublimis, 'lifted up').   1671 *regorged*: gorged to repletion.   1672
Chaunting: chanting, singing praises to.   1680 *Unweetingly*: un-
wittingly.

As their own ruin on themselves to invite,
Insensate left, or to sense reprobate,
And with blindness internal struck.

Semichorus. But he though blind of sight,
  Despised and thought extinguish'd quite,
  With inward eyes illuminated
  His fiery virtue roused   1690
  From under ashes into sudden flame,
  And as an ev'ning Dragon came,
  Assailant on the perched roosts,
  And nests in order ranged
  Of tame villatic Fowl; but as an Eagle
  His cloudless thunder bolted on their heads.
  So virtue giv'n for lost,
  Depress'd, and overthrown, as seem'd,
  Like that self-begotten bird
  In the *Arabian* woods embost,   1700
  That no second knows nor third,
  And lay erewhile a Holocaust,
  From out her ashy womb now teem'd
  Revives, reflourishes, then vigorous most
  When most unactive deem'd;
  And though her body die, her fame survives,
  A secular bird ages of lives.

1685 *Insensate*: devoid of understanding.   *to sense reprobate*: intolerant
or incapable of reason.   1690 *virtue*: physical strength, but with the
Latin meanings of 'spirit' or 'courage'.   1692–6 *Dragon*: serpent
(Latin, *draco*).   1695 *villatic*: farmyard (Latin, *villa*, 'farm').   1696
His cloudless thunder: his thunder from a clear sky, i.e. unexpected.   *bolted*:
shot forth as an arrow.   1697 *giv'n for lost*: accounted lost.   1699
that self-begotten bird: i.e. the Phoenix.   1700 *embost*: embosked, i.e.
surrounded by woods, hidden.   1702 *Holocaust*: a burnt offering
offered whole.   1703 *teem'd*: brought to birth.   1707 *A secular
bird*: a bird lasting many ages or centuries (Latin, *saeculum*).

Manoa. Come, come, no time for lamentation now,
  Nor much more cause. *Samson* hath quit himself
  Like *Samson*, and heroicly hath finish'd   1710
  A life Heroic, on his Enemies
  Fully revenged, hath left them years of mourning,
  And lamentation to the Sons of *Caphtor*
  Through all *Philistian* bounds; to *Israel*
  Honour hath left, and freedom, let but them
  Find courage to lay hold on this occasion,
  To himself and Father's house eternal fame;
  And which is best and happiest yet, all this
  With God not parted from him, as was fear'd,
  But favouring and assisting to the end.   1720
  Nothing is here for tears, nothing to wail
  Or knock the breast, no weakness, no contempt,
  Dispraise, or blame, nothing but well and fair,
  And what may quiet us in a death so noble.
  Let us go find the body where it lies
  Soak'd in his enemies' blood, and from the stream
  With lavers pure and cleansing herbs wash off
  The clotted gore. I with what speed the while
  (*Gaza* is not in plight to say us nay)
  Will send for all my kindred, all my friends   1730
  To fetch him hence and solemnly attend
  With silent obsequy and funeral train
  Home to his Father's house: there will I build him
  A Monument, and plant it round with shade
  Of Laurel ever green, and branching Palm,
  With all his Trophies hung, and Acts enroll'd

1709 *quit himself*: acquitted himself.   1714 *bounds*: borders.   1722
knock the breast: i.e. in sign of mourning.   1727 *lavers*: vessels for
bathing.   1728 *I with what speed the while*: I in the meantime with all
speed.   1729 'The Philistines are not in a position to hinder us.'
1732 *train*: procession.

In copious Legend, or sweet Lyric Song.
Thither shall all the valiant youth resort,
And from his memory inflame their breasts
To matchless valour and adventures high: 1740
The Virgins also shall on feastful days
Visit his Tomb with flowers, only bewailing
His lot unfortunate in nuptial choice,
From whence captivity and loss of eyes.

Chorus. All is best, though we oft doubt,
 What th' unsearchable dispose
Of highest wisdom brings about,
And ever best found in the close.
Oft he seems to hide his face,
But unexpectedly returns   1750
And to his faithful Champion hath in place
Bore witness gloriously; whence *Gaza* mourns
And all that band them to resist
His uncontrollable intent;
His servants he with new acquist
Of true experience from this great event
With peace and consolation hath dismiss'd,
And calm of mind, all passion spent.

THE END

1737 *copious Legend*: full inscription.   1738 *the valiant youth*: the
young fighting men.   1746 *dispose*: disposition or ordering of things.
1749 *hide his face*: turn away in anger or indifference.   1751 *in place*:
in the right place, at the right moment.   1753 *band them*: form themselves into a band or league.   1755 *acquist*: increase, acquisition.

NOTES

SAMSON AGONISTES: *agonistes* is Greek for 'a combatant in the games' (*ἀγών*, a contest). Used of competitors in the public athletic contests of ancient Greece, here it refers to Samson's display of strength at the festival of Dagon, and thus indicates which episode in the hero's life the drama is to present. In the form of this title Milton follows Greek examples, such as those of Aeschylus in his *Prometheus Bound* and of Sophocles in *Oedipus Coloneus* ('Oedipus at Colonus'). Italian epic poets of the Renaissance followed the convention, as Ariosto in the *Orlando Furioso*, 'Orlando Mad', and Tasso in *Gerusalemme Liberata*, 'Jerusalem Delivered'. Milton's own epics have similar titles, and his earlier project for treating the subject of *Paradise Lost* in dramatic form was to be called *Adam Unparadiz'd*.

OF THAT SORT OF DRAMATIC POEM WHICH IS CALL'D TRAGEDY

This preface has two purposes, both indicated in its opening sentence: the first, to assert the spiritual value of tragic drama; the second, to claim that ancient Greek tragedy is the only proper model for such drama, and that Milton's poem follows it in all essential features.

3. ARISTOTLE. Milton here paraphrases part of the definition of tragedy from Aristotle's *Poetics* which he quoted in Greek and Latin on his title-page. It may be noted that he cites Aristotle's definition as what it was, an observation on the ancient Greek dramas, and not a rule according to which they were constructed.

7–11. *Nor is Nature wanting . . . humours.* This explanation of the workings of Aristotle's 'catharsis' had been offered by the Italian Minturno in his *Art of Poetry* (1564). It reminds us that what was first called 'homoeopathy' at the end of the eighteenth century was a system of medical practice which went back to much earlier times, based on the principle that 'likes are cured by likes'; diseases are therefore treated, on this system, by small doses of drugs which would normally produce symptoms like those of the disease in question. In translating *katharsis* by *lustratio* on his title-page Milton followed

other sixteenth-century scholars, who introduced this Latin word
to suggest a ritual or ceremonial purification (see W. R. Parker,
Milton's Debt to Greek Tragedy in Samson Agonistes (Baltimore,
1937), p. 68). But in putting forward the 'homoeopathic' explanation in his commentary, Milton makes a very characteristic choice.
He chooses to interpret the spiritual effects of tragedy in terms of
individual experience, claiming that there is a scientific explanation
of the way in which our emotions are 'purged' by the representation
of human sufferings which tragedy offers. This is in accordance with
his rational approach to religious dogma and practice. The interpretation of 'catharsis' as a ritual or ceremonial purification would,
on the other hand, imply a different conception of spiritual experience, one in which the individual would be less important and
the community more important.

11–29. *Hence Philosophers* . . . CHRIST SUFFERING. Milton here
begins to support his appeal to reason by an appeal to various
authorities, both Pagan and Christian.

13–14. *The Apostle* PAUL. St. Paul quoted the verse 'Evil commu-
nications corrupt good manners', but probably without realizing that
it was anything more than a current Greek proverb. It is not now
attributed with certainty to Euripides.

16. PARÆUS: David Paræus, a German theologian whose work on
the Book of Revelations was published in 1628. Milton had referred
to it in the Preface of Book II of *The Reason of Church Government*
(1641), where he calls the Apocalypse of St. John 'the majestick
image of a high and stately Tragedy, shutting up and intermingling
her solemn Scenes and Acts with a sevenfold *Chorus* of halleluja's
and harping symphonies: and this my opinion the grave autority
of *Pareus* . . . is sufficient to confirm'.

21. DIONYSIUS. 431–367 B.C. As tyrant of Syracuse in Sicily, he
patronized the arts and wrote a tragedy which was awarded a prize
by the Athenians at the festival of Dionysus (the god from whom
the tyrant derived his name).

22. AUGUSTUS CÆSAR. Suetonius tells of this literary venture
(ii. 85).

24. SENECA: Roman orator and writer (5–4 B.C.–A.D. 65). Milton's
caution in asserting his authorship of the ten tragedies was justified

by the state of scholarship in his time. They are now generally attributed to this author.

27. GREGORY NAZIANZEN: Bishop of Constantinople (A.D. 325–90). The tragedy referred to was, however, probably written by a twelfth-century Byzantine Greek. It was well known in the sixteenth century, and was referred to by Stephen Gosson in his attack upon drama in *The Schoole of Abuse* (1579).

29–37. *This is mention'd . . . the people*. Tragedy, like all forms of drama, was held in 'small esteem, or rather infamy' by many educated Protestants as well as by popular Puritan opinion. Elizabethan and Stuart drama had undergone constant attack from the Puritans, and had been protected only by the favour of the Court. Milton makes the point, however, that the popular drama was itself to blame for the offence it gave to serious-minded people. His opinion of Elizabethan drama in general would have been that of Sidney: 'Our Tragidies and Commedies, not without cause cryed out against, observing rules neither of honest civilitie, nor skilfull Poetrie' (*The Defence of Poetrie*, 1595). It is certain, however, that the Puritans were not offended only by the artistic licence of the Elizabethan and later drama: they would not have been satisfied with less than the suppression of all dramatic representations, as of most other forms of art.

38. *Prologue*. The word is used here to mean an apology or preface to a work of art, like the epistle to the reader prefixed to Martial's Epigrams. Milton disregards the technical use of the term by Aristotle to mean 'the whole of that part of a tragedy which precedes the entrance of the chorus' (*Poetics* xii). But he may have had in mind such prologues in verse as were common on the Restoration stage and had also been used by Marlowe, Shakespeare (*Troilus and Cressida* and *Henry V*) and Ben Jonson.

41–42. *thus much before-hand may be Epistled*. Milton adds what he thinks necessary to the understanding of the form of his poem, which he emphasizes was never meant for the stage.

42–43. *that* CHORUS . . . *not ancient only but modern*. The Chorus was an essential feature of ancient Greek tragedy; in fact Greek tragedy is usually supposed to have sprung from songs and dances performed at religious festivals.

44. *still in use among the* ITALIANS. Throughout his explanations Milton adduces the authority of Italian literature as equal to that of Greek and Roman. This is in accordance with the tractate *Of Education* (1644), where Milton speaks of the use of criticism, 'that sublime Art which in *Aristotles Poetics*, in *Horace*, and the *Italian* Commentaries of *Castelvetro*, *Tasso*, *Mazzoni*, and others, teaches what the laws are of a true *Epic* Poem, what of a *Dramatic*, what of a *Lyric*, what Decorum is, which is the grand master-piece to observe'. The expression 'still in use' is somewhat misleading, since it suggests that the use of the Chorus in sixteenth- and seventeenth-century Italian dramas continued a tradition ascending to ancient times. There was no such continuous tradition, and the appearance of the Chorus in such Renaissance tragedies as Trissino's *Sofonisba* and Tasso's *Torrismondo* was the result of a literary imitation of ancient Greek and Senecan tragedy.

48. MONOSTROPHIC: consisting of a single strophe or stanza, i.e. without a recurrent pattern.

APOLELYMENON: a Greek word meaning 'freed', i.e. released from the obligation to carry a repeated metrical pattern.

49. STROPHE, ANTISTROPHE, *or* EPODE. Milton rightly refers these Greek metrical divisions to the music to which the Greek tragic Chorus sang. As they sang the *strophe* they moved in dance from right to left; moving in a corresponding dance from left to right they then sang a corresponding verse, the *antistrophe*; having returned to their original position, they stood still to sing the *epode*, which was in a different form of verse and to another tune. Many Renaissance and later imitations of Greek tragedy attempt to preserve these metrical divisions, despite their lack of meaning without the original music and movement.

53. ALLÆOSTROPHA: having strophes or stanzas of varied form. For a discussion of the structure of Milton's choruses see Appendix A, *On the Verse*.

53-57. *Division into Act and Scene . . . the fifth Act*. The most important point here is that, although the tragedy is printed as a poem, i.e. without the act and scene divisions necessary for stage production, it is nevertheless constructed on the Greek dramatic principles. The notion of strictly 'five acts' as normal in tragedy was unknown to the Greek dramatists (though the choruses generally divide Greek tragedies into four or five acts or 'episodes'); it was, however, established in Elizabethan drama, deriving probably from the tragedies of Seneca (see T. W. Baldwin, *Shakspere's Five-Act Structure*, Urbana, 1947).

Samson Agonistes can be analysed in a way which corresponds closely to Greek precedents. The poem begins with a *prologos*, the 114 lines of Samson's soliloquy. This is followed by a *parodos*, the 61 lines spoken by the Chorus when it first enters, and before it addresses Samson. The dialogue which follows between Samson and the Chorus (176–292) is the first *epeisodion*, and is followed by the first *stasimon*, or choral ode (293–325). The Chorus remains on the stage throughout, and comments on each episode in a *stasimon*, besides taking a certain part in the dialogue. The second *epeisodion* begins when Manoa enters (326). The third *epeisodion* is the interview between Samson and Dalila (710–1009); the fourth, that between Samson and Harapha (1061–1267); the fifth, the two visits of the Philistine official, ends with Samson's departure to the festival of Dagon (1301–1426). When Manoa re-enters, the *exodos* of the play begins (1441), and continues until the Messenger has given the story of Samson's death. The comments of the Chorus and Manoa form the *kommos* (1660–1758), which concludes the play.

58–65. *Of the style and uniformity . . . Tragedy*. Milton's reference to the three great Attic dramatists, as well as an analysis of his tragedy, shows that he is following no one dramatist, and still less any one play. The parts of *Samson Agonistes* may be given Greek names, and it can be seen to be constructed according to Greek principles. But it is equally important to realize that Milton has allowed his subject, and his conception of its meaning, to dictate the final shape of his drama.

58–59. *that commonly call'd the Plot, whether intricate or explicit*. Aristotle declared the plot to be the most important of the six elements he distinguished in tragic drama, and the most difficult for a dramatist to master. The distinction between 'intricate' and 'explicit' probably refers to Aristotle's distinction between 'complex' and 'simple' plots. 'Aristotle called plots in which there was no sudden reversal in the fortune of the hero from happiness to misery, or from misery to happiness and back again, simple' (Merritt

Hughes, *Paradise Regained, the Minor Poems and Samson Agonistes* (New York, 1937), p. 540 n.). Aristotle preferred complex plots, i.e. 'with *peripeteia* and *anagnorisis*'. 'A *peripeteia* happens, not when there is a mere change of fortune, but when an intention or action brings about the opposite of what was meant. Now Milton made *Samson Agonistes* answer so closely to this interpretation of *peripeteia* that I believe it was his own interpretation. . . . The essence of the plot of *Samson* is that all the actions should lead whither they had not seemed to lead' (E. M. W. Tillyard, *Milton* (London, 1930), p. 343).

65. *The circumscription of time.* The 'unity of time' indicated here was not precisely an 'ancient rule', though mentioned as a general practice by Aristotle (*Poetics* v). It was first put forward as a principle by sixteenth-century Italian critics. It is true that Aeschylus, Sophocles, and Euripides generally made 12, or at the most 24, hours the supposed duration of the action of their plays; but this seems to have been a natural growth rather than a rule, and it was subject to variations.

THE ARGUMENT

The story of Samson is given in the Old Testament, in the Book of Judges, chaps. xiii–xvi. In choosing for dramatic treatment the last phase of Samson's life, Milton had to devise a brief series of actions and discussions, which he calls the 'economy, or disposition of the fable'. The Argument describes these.

While presenting only the few hours before Samson's death, the poem refers to almost all the events of his life. But Milton omits certain details which might detract from Samson's value as a tragic hero. For example, he does not mention the boisterous revenge he took on the Philistines in setting fire to their crops by means of fire-brands tied to foxes' tails (Judges xv. 4, 5). He touches only lightly on the riddle, and the subsequent relations of Samson with the woman of Timnath (Judges xiv. 12–20 and xv. 1, 2). He has modified the impression of Samson's relations with women (Judges xvi. 1), and presents the connexion with Dalila as a marriage. By disregarding the statement that Samson 'judged Israel in the days of the Philistines twenty years' (Judges xv. 20), he has made his hero more lonely and independent. By making Manoa a wealthy man (1479) he has enabled the father to play a part of some importance in his son's last days, and he has also increased the dignity of the story, in accordance with the Aristotelian and Renaissance view that tragedy must depict the affairs of the great. Such modifications fall in with the practice of the Greeks. The audience in ancient Greece knew the substance of the story to be presented, and would know what climax or catastrophe to expect in any particular phase; but the dramatist was allowed, or rather expected, to produce his own version of events, and his own vision of their meaning.

THE PLAY

Lines 1–114

Samson enters, led by a guide, to whom he speaks the first eleven lines, and who then leaves him, without having spoken. (The Greeks called such characters 'silent actors'; Dalila's 'damsel train' similarly accompany her without speaking (710–1009).) Samson in a long soliloquy gives the most important elements of the dramatic situation. He mentions at once what gives him this opportunity for rest and thought: a Philistine feast in honour of Dagon (12–17). Thus Milton states at the beginning the circumstance which gives rise to the final catastrophe. Samson describes the torment of mind which he cannot escape, and contrasts his present wretched state with the promises which had preceded his birth, and with the instructions given to his parents to rear him as one dedicated to God and destined to do great deeds for his country. What can God have meant by such preparations, if the future champion was to be defeated in the end (23–42)? But Samson reminds himself that his own conduct is enough to account for the apparent failure of the prophecies. His weakness of will revealed to his wife the source of his strength, thus showing how useless physical strength is without wisdom (46–57). God's gift to him of strength alone was of little value, and therefore suitably dependent on so slight a thing as his hair. He checks an impulse to question God's justice here (60–62), but goes on to lament that strength has been to him so fatal a gift, leading to so many disasters, and among them, and worst of all, the loss of his sight (63–79). The rest of his speech expresses the miseries of blindness, which adds so greatly to his other sufferings; as before, he tends to question the wisdom and justice of God, asking why, if light is so needful and blessed a thing, it should be so easy to deprive man of his sight (90–97). As Samson's emotion becomes more intense the soliloquy quickens in pace (66–79), and finally becomes a lyrical lament (80–109). This he breaks off (110), hearing the approach of the Chorus, who he fears may be Philistines. The verse in the last few lines (110–14) therefore changes back to the blank verse which is Milton's representation of ordinary speech.

This long speech, which may be called a *prologos*, gives on the one hand the essential facts of Samson's situation, and on the other, a picture of his state of mind. He is torn by remorse and assailed by doubts; but he does not lose sight of his own responsibility for his fall, and so will not rebel against God. His mind is in no state for action, but at least clings to its sense of right and wrong.

1–2. In the opening scene of Sophocles' *Oedipus at Colonus* the blind Oedipus is led on by his daughter Antigone; the blind prophet Tiresias is also led by his daughter in the *Phoenissae* of Euripides (ll. 834–5).

5. *servile toil*. 'Exactly the Latin "*servilis labor*", toil which slaves perform' (Churton Collins).

6. *enjoin'd me*. See 1342.

13. *Sea-Idol*. Dagon the fish-god, described in *P.L.* i. 462:

> DAGON his Name, Sea Monster, upward Man
> And downward Fish:

His overthrow by the Ark of the Covenant is told in 1 Samuel v. 4.

16. *the popular noise*. For 'popular' used in this, the Latin, sense see also *P.L.* ii. 313–14.

23–29. The prophecies before Samson's birth are related in Judges xiii, the first being to his mother: 'And the LORD appeared unto the woman, and said unto her, Behold now, thou *art* barren, and bearest not: but thou shalt conceive, and bear a son' (verse 3). The angel appeared a second time to both parents, and then vanished in the flame of the sacrifice offered in gratitude by Manoa (Judges xiii. 19–20).

27. *charioting*. Josephus says that 'the angel ascended openly, in their sight, up to heaven, by means of the smoke as by a vehicle' (*Antiquities*, v. vii). Milton is probably thinking also of Elijah's ascent to Heaven in a chariot of fire (2 Kings ii. 11).

30–32. Manoa and his wife were told to dedicate their child to God as a future champion of His people: 'and no rasor shall come on his head: for the child shall be a Nazarite unto God from the womb: and he shall begin to deliver Israel out of the hand of the Philistines' (Judges xiii. 5). The rule of life to be observed by Nazarites is given in Numbers vi.

31. *separate*. The word 'Nazarite' came from a root meaning 'to separate', because Nazarites, men or women, were to 'separate *themselves* to vow a vow of a Nazarite, to separate *themselves* unto the LORD' (Numbers vi. 2).

33. *Captived*. The accent is on the second syllable, as in

> Thus when as *Guyon Furor* had captiv'd
> > (*The Faerie Queene*, II. iv. 16).

See also 694.

34. *gaze*. See also 567.

38. *Promise was*. The promise was made by the angel in Judges xiii. 5.

41. GAZA: once the capital city of the Philistines; called *Azza* in 147.

at the Mill with slaves. Mills were often worked by man-power or by animals in the East. Convicts or other prisoners were obvious sources of such labour. See also 1162–3.

48. *bereft me*. See also 85. 'Bereave' and 'bereft' were more often used with 'of':

> Madam, you have bereft me of all words
> > (*Merchant of Venice*, III. ii. 177).

But this could be omitted, as in *P.L.* x. 918:

> Bereave me not . . . thy gentle looks, thy aid . . .

53–54. The uselessness of strength without wisdom was a moral commonplace in classical and medieval literature.

70. *the prime work of God*. 'And God said, Let there be light: and there was light' (Genesis i. 3). Cf. 83–85.

87. ' "*Luna silens*", or "silent moon", was a Latin phrase for the absence of moonlight' (Masson). But this technical meaning does not wholly account for the effect of 'silent'. As Churton Collins

says, 'By an interchange of metaphors not uncommon in classical poetry, a word which properly applies only to sound is here applied to sight, and silent = dark, devoid of light'. He compares Dante, *Inferno*, i. 60:

> Mi ripingeva là, dove il sol tace.

89. *vacant interlunar cave*. 'Vacant' retains its Latin meaning of 'empty' or 'at leisure', as in Milton's own translation of Horace, *Odes* I. v:

> Who always vacant, always amiable
> Hopes thee;

But perhaps the line depends for its effect partly on the apparent contradiction between the cave's 'emptiness' and the idea that it also contains the moon. These slight shocks are an important feature of Milton's style. The cave itself might be thought to be the bowl of the night-sky, empty of the moon. But in ancient times the moon was really supposed to retire into a cave between her disappearance as the old moon and her reappearance as the new.

95. *obvious*. For this Latin sense of the word, cf. *P.L.* viii. 504.

96–97. There is a strange intensity and daring in this idea.

106. *obnoxious*. For this Latin sense of the word, cf. *P.L.* ix. 170, 1094.

111. *steering*. Compare the image of Mercy:

> With radiant feet the tissued clouds down steering,
> > (*On the Morning of Christ's Nativity*, 146).

Lines 115–75

The Chorus enters, but at first keeps at some distance from Samson. It comments on his wretched appearance, contrasting it with his former strength and glorious deeds (124–50). Which is more deserving of pity, his captivity or his blindness, itself a form of captivity (151–63)? Could there be a better example of the un-certainty of human happiness? For this fall from former prosperity and fame is that of a truly great man, not one whose greatness was founded merely on privilege or inheritance (164–75).—The sub-stance of this chorus is similar to that of Samson's soliloquy which precedes it. Throughout the poem Milton thus uses the choruses to prolong and intensify the emotions aroused by the preceding dialogue.

118. *diffused*. The literal Latin meaning of 'diffused' is 'poured out'. In Elizabethan English the word (generally spelt 'defused') meant 'loose, disordered', as in:

> . . . But grow like savages,—as soldiers will,
> That nothing do but meditate on blood,—
> To swearing and stern looks, diffus'd attire,
> And every thing that seems unnatural.
>
> (*Henry V*, v. ii. 59–62).

On this and the next line Masson comments: 'probably . . . a recollection from Ovid, *Epist.* III. iii. 8:

> Fusaque erant toto languida membra toro'.

122. *habit*. See also 1305.

weeds. This Anglo-Saxon word survives only in the alliterative 'widow's weeds'.

128. In Judges xiv. 5–6 Samson meets a young lion, which 'roared against him . . . and he rent him as he would have rent a kid'.

132. *Cuirass*. A piece of body-armour, originally of leather. It reached down to the waist, consisting of a breast-plate and a back-plate. The breast-plate alone was sometimes called a cuirass.

133. CHALYBEAN. Here 'Chalýbean'. The Chalybes were famous iron-workers of Scythia.

frock of mail: coat of mail, i.e. armour composed of interlaced rings or chain-work.

134. *Adamantean Proof*. 'Adamant', meaning literally 'unsubduable', was used in the ancient world to describe steel of the hardest kind; but in the Middle Ages and later it was used to mean diamond or loadstone. Satan's shield is of adamant, in *P.L.* vi. 254.

137. *tools*. Compare: 'Draw thy toole, here comes two of the house of Montagues' (*Romeo and Juliet*, I. i. 28–29).

138. ASCALONITE. Accent 'Ascálonite'. Ashkelon or Askelon was one of the chief cities of the Philistines, lying on the coast between Ashdod and Gaza.

139. *ramp*. Compare the heraldic phrase 'a lion rampant' (French, *ramper*). See also *P.L.* iv. 343.

142. *what trivial weapon*: the jawbone of an ass which Samson found, 'and slew a thousand men therewith. And Samson said, with the jawbone of an ass, heaps upon heaps, with the jaw of an ass have I slain a thousand men' (Judges xv. 15–16). In 'trivial' Milton combines the usual meaning of 'slight, commonplace' with the literal Latin meaning of 'picked up at the cross-roads' (*trivium*).

144. *fore-skins*: used for the Philistines because they were an uncircumcized race.

PALESTINE: used in the special sense of 'Philistia'.

145. RAMATH-LECHI. The popular etymology of this place-name was 'the lifting up of the jawbone' or 'the casting away of the jawbone'. 'He cast away the jaw-bone out of his hand and called that place Ramath-lechi' (Judges xv. 17).

147. AZZA: another name for Gaza. This exploit of Samson is told in Judges xvi. 3.

148. HEBRON: a hill-town of Judah, directly inland from Gaza. The name was supposed to derive from one Arba, ancestor of the giants called Anakim. See Numbers xiii. 33; and 1080.

149. *No journey of a Sabbath day*. Jewish religious precepts limited a journey on the Sabbath to three-quarters of a mile (Exodus xvi. 29). Hebron was thirty or forty miles from Gaza.

150. *Like whom the Gentiles feign to bear up Heav'n*. i.e. like him whom, &c. The term 'Gentiles' included all non-Jewish peoples; here the Greeks are meant (see also 500). The Greek story Milton refers to is that of Atlas, who in the Odyssey (i. 52) is said to carry the great columns which keep Heaven and Earth apart. Later Greek traditions made him the leader of the Titans in their war against Zeus; when they were defeated he was condemned to the labour of bearing Heaven on his head and hands. By such allusions to 'the Gentiles' Milton introduces into his poem those references to Graeco-Roman mythology which were felt to be necessary in neo-classical poetry. For an adverse criticism of this procedure see Dr. Johnson's essay in *The Rambler*, No. 140.

157. This parenthesis is a comment on the whole statement from

156 to 163. That the soul was imprisoned in the body was a common idea in Pythagorean and Platonic philosophy.

161. *To incorporate.* Cf. *P.L.* x. 816.

162. *alas.* If punctuation is added to this interjection it spoils the flow of the lines.

163. *visual beam.* The faculty of sight was sometimes imagined to take the form of a ray of light issuing from the eye. Compare:

> Our eye-beames twisted, and did thred
> Our eyes, upon one double string;
> > (Donne, *The Extasie*).

165. *Since man on earth unparallel'd.* 'Since man on earth' recalls the well-known Latin construction (*post urbem conditam*, 'since the founding of the city'), which Milton imitated in:

> For never since created man,
> Met such imbodied force,
> > (*P.L.* i. 573–4).

169. *pitch.* This word can signify either relative *height* or relative *depth* (cf. Latin *altus*).

172. *the sphere of fortune.* The goddess Fortune, who ruled over men's worldly prosperity or adversity, was imagined as standing on a rotating globe or a wheel, which symbolized the instability of her dispensation. In medieval art great men were sometimes depicted as placed at various points, high or low, on the rim of Fortune's wheel, which in turning raised them up or cast them down.

Lines 176–292

Samson says he can hear voices, but cannot distinguish the words. The Chorus coming nearer introduces itself to him as a band of his friends and neighbours, fellow-members of the tribe of Dan, who have come to lament his misfortunes and, if possible, comfort him (178–86). Samson welcomes them as true friends, since they are faithful in misfortune, and immediately declares himself ashamed of his past folly. Yet, he asks, was it really my fault that God gave me so much strength and so little wisdom (196–209)? The Chorus forbids him to criticize God's providence, adding that even wise

men have been led astray by women (210–12). Yet, they continue,
as in all fairness, it is certainly a matter for wonder that Samson
should have chosen to marry Philistine women rather than women of
his own race and faith (213–18). Samson, however, replies that his
two marriages were prompted by God, and that he had in mind the
opportunities they might give him to act against the Philistines, the
oppressors of his people. Dalila was in any case less the cause of his
downfall than he himself (219–36). The Chorus, while admitting
that Samson always showed a praiseworthy zeal in the national
cause, points out that nevertheless he has not succeeded in liberating
the Israelites from the Philistine rule (237–40). For this, Samson
replies, the Israelite leaders must blame themselves, since they failed
to support his enterprises: for instance, the tribe of Judah did not
rally to him at Etham, or seize their chance to attack the Philistines
after he had defeated them single-handed at Ramath-Lechi (241–62).
But this supine cowardice is characteristic of nations which have
grown corrupt in servitude: they are only too ready to betray those
who seek to free them (263–89). The Chorus agrees that the
Israelites have often so acted towards their greatest champions
(277–89). Samson says they may now add his case to the others; not
that his personal fate is important, but that in rejecting him the
people have rejected God's offer of freedom (290–2).

181. *From* ESHTAOL *and* ZORA'*s fruitful Vale*. Manoa was 'a certain
man of Zorah, of the family of the Danites' (Judges xiii. 2). The
same chapter of Judges tells of Samson's boyhood in this region:
'And the spirit of the LORD began to move him at times in the camp
of Dan between Zorah and Eshtaol' (verse 25). The two villages
have been identified as lying between the territories of Dan and
Judah.

182–5. 'or if (which would be better) we might bring you advice
or consolation, it would be as ointment to your wounds, for apt
words have power', &c.

184–6. The power of words to soothe grief or anger was proverbial in Greek and Latin writers. Merritt Hughes cites the remark
of Ocean in Aeschylus' *Prometheus Bound*, 379:

> Know'st thou not this, Prometheus, that mild words
> Are medicines of fierce wrath?

184. *swage.* Compare:

> Nor wanting power to mitigate and swage
> With solemn touches troubled thoughts,
> (P.L. i. 556–7).

185. *tumours.* From the literal Latin sense of 'swellings' this word was often used to mean movements of passion or a troubled state of mind.

189–90. *Superscription*: literally the writing which denotes the value of a coin.

191–2. There are countless ancient and modern parallels to this reflection on 'fair weather' friends.

197. *heave the head.* Compare:

> Rise, rise, and heave thy rosy head
> From thy coral-paven bed,
> (Comus, 885–6).

203. *proverb'd.* See Psalm lxix. 11 and Job xvii. 6.

209. *drove me transverse.* The metaphor of a ship is continued from 199.

212. *pretend they ne'er so wise.* Cf. *P.L.* x. 896–908.

219. TIMNA. Timnath was a Philistine city on the northern frontier of Judah. 'And Samson went down to Timnath, and saw a woman in Timnath of the daughters of the Philistines' (Judges xiv. 1). Milton drops the 'th' as an awkward sound.

220. *not my parents, that I sought to wed.* See 224 n.

222. *motion'd.* Cf. *P.L.* ix. 229.

224. *that by occasion hence.* 'But his father and mother knew not that it *was* of the LORD, that he sought an occasion against the Philistines' (Judges xiv. 4).

226. *divinely.* Cf. *P.L.* viii. 900.

229. SOREC. 'And it came to pass afterward, that he loved a woman in the valley of Sorek, whose name was Delilah' (Judges xvi. 4). Sorek may be Surar, in the neighbourhood of Ekron (see note to 981).

230. *accomplish'd*. The word suggests calculation and practice, and therefore, in some cases, cunning. Milton may also intend a double meaning: 'she who accomplished my capture'.

235. *peal*. See 906. 'And it came to pass, when she pressed him daily with her words, and urged him, so that his soul was vexed unto death; that he told her all his heart' (see Judges xvi. 16, 17).

240. ISRAEL. This was originally an alternative name for Jacob, father of the twelve patriarchs who were the reputed ancestors of the twelve tribes of Israel. When the Jews referred to themselves as 'Israel' or 'the children of Israel', the word kept its quality of an individual proper name, as it does in this passage.

252–3. Samson's first differences with the Philistines came to a head after his destruction of their crops, as a result of his marriage to the woman of Timnath (Judges xiv. 1–7). The Philistines then attacked him: 'And he smote them hip and thigh with a great slaughter: and he went and dwelt in the top of the rock Etam' (Judges xv. 8).

256–64. These events are related in Judges xv. 9–15.

258. *on some conditions*. The conditions were that the men of Judah should deliver Samson bound into the hands of the Philistines, but should not themselves attack him.

263. *a trivial weapon*. See 142 and n.

265–7. The men of Judah were at this time subject to the Philistines (Judges xv. 11). The site of the Philistine city of Gath is not known with certainty.

268–76. Milton intends this judgement to be applied to the English nation, which in recalling Charles II had betrayed the cause of freedom for which the Civil War had been fought.

278. SUCCOTH: a place near the Jordan, not far south of the confluence of the Jabbok.

PENUEL: or Peniel, a place east of the Jordan; it had a strong tower or castle, and was of considerable strategic importance. When Gideon's forces were pursuing the defeated kings of Midian across the Jordan, they were refused provisions by their fellow Israelites living at these two places (Judges viii. 5, 6).

281. MADIAN: the form of Midian used in the Vulgate or Latin Bible.

282-9. 'Jephtha the Gileadite', after asserting Hebrew power against 'the children of Amman', was challenged by the men of Ephraim, who professed to be angry that he had not consulted them beforehand. Jephtha and the men of Gilead then took possession of the passages of the river Jordan and, identifying the Ephraimites who wished to cross over by their inability to pronounce the word Shibboleth correctly, they massacred them. See Judges xii. 4-6.

283-5. The reference is to the long message sent by Jephtha to 'the king of the children of Amman', arguing that the Israelites had by conquest acquired a prescriptive right to the land of the Amorites (Judges xi. 14-27).

Lines 293-325

The Chorus asserts the justice of God, which can never be questioned without wrong and confusion (293-306). Being infinite, God cannot be bound even by his own ordinances for men. He may release whom he wishes from his laws forbidding marriage between Jews and Gentiles, as he presumably released Samson in inspiring him to marry the woman of Timnath, though this was also against Samson's vow of purity as a Nazarite (307-21). Reason must be held in check in considering God's ways: yet the Chorus points out that Samson's first wife was 'unclean' only according to the Mosaic law, not guilty in a moral sense; and her unchastity after marriage has no bearing on the rightness or wrongness of his choice (322-5). The Chorus breaks off to announce Manoa's entry.

295. *who think not God.* 'Think' in this sense is an imitation of a Latin and Greek idiom (Greek νομίζειν).

298. *But the heart of the Fool*: an allusion to Psalm xiv. 1: 'The fool hath said in his heart, There is no God.'

301. *As to his own edicts found contradicting.* Note the play upon words of which Milton is fond: compare for example:

> hee to be aveng'd,
> And to repaire his numbers thus impair'd
> (*P.L.* ix. 143-4).

See also 1278.

303. *his glory's diminution*: Churton Collins explains: 'A Latin idiom and a Latin phrase. "Majestatem populi Romani minuere" (Cic. de Orat. ii. 39) is the same as "crimen laesae majestatis", that is "high treason"; so here, regardless of committing high treason against God.'

312. *National obstriction*: the restraints put upon the Jews by the Mosaic law, and particularly the prohibition of marriages with Gentiles (Deuteronomy vii. 3).

321. *Unclean.* According to the Mosaic law all Gentiles were 'unclean'; but Milton a few lines later indicates that 'uncleanness' cannot be a matter of race or birth, but of act (324).

324. *verdit.* Milton's spelling preserves the old pronunciation. 'Moral verdict' would be a judgement based on men's individual actions, not on their racial or religious standing.

Lines 326–605

Manoa enters, to lament his son's downfall (340–72), and to reprove him for the encouragement it has given to God's enemies (420–47). Samson once more accepts full responsibility for his own disgrace (373–419) and acknowledges that he has enabled the God of the Philistines to triumph (448–59). But he affirms that the true God, now face to face with Dagon, will yet manifest his power (460–71). Manoa reveals that he has approached the Philistines with proposals for his son's ransom; but Samson declares that he would rather endure the punishment which he has deserved (481–520). Why should he wish for further life, he asks, since he has so fallen from his former state of glory (521–40)? The Chorus tries to console him by praising his abstinence in the past, but Samson points out that abstinence from wine was of little avail, since it was not accompanied by abstinence from sexual indulgence, which led to his ruin (541–76). Manoa proceeds to argue that Samson must not use his strength, now restored, to serve God's enemies: if he accepts his release, God may well restore his sight, thus making possible further heroic deeds (577–89). But Samson feels this to be impossible: his active life is over, death must be near (590–8). Manoa is unconvinced, and goes off to pursue the possibility of ransom (599–605).

Throughout the dialogue Milton scatters passages which complete the story (381–409; 522–31; 541–52). By introducing the possibility of ransom (his own invention) he obtains a two-fold dramatic effect: since the question remains to be settled, it impels the plot forward; and, by giving Samson a clear impression of what is after all the best he can hope for, it precipitates in him a deeper sense of sorrow and a deeper conviction of his guilt. Yet, although he condemns and abandons himself (or perhaps *because* he does so), he believes and prophesies that God will yet triumph. In drama it is always understood that prophecies will be shown to be either frustrated or fulfilled; so that this is another factor inducing expectation and suspense.

332–7. This explains why Manoa enters some time after the Chorus: he set out at about the same time, but walked more slowly.

339. *erst*: formerly.

357. *pomp.* See 436 n.

373. *Appoint not heav'nly disposition.* There seems to be no exact parallel to the use of 'appoint' in the sense of 'call in question'; but this meaning suggests itself strongly (see also 210).

377. *profaned.* To 'profane' in Latin meant to 'disclose a sacred secret'.

380. CANAANITE. The Philistines were not strictly speaking Canaanites, but this term was extended to include all who were rivals or opponents to the Israelites in their mission to conquer Palestine.

382–7. The story of the riddle which Samson propounded to the thirty Philistine groomsmen present at his wedding is told in Judges xiv:

'So his father went down unto the woman: and Samson made there a feast; for so used the young men to do. And it came to pass, when they saw him, that they brought thirty companions to be with him.

'And Samson said unto them, I will now put a riddle unto you: if ye can certainly declare it me within the seven days of the feast, and find it out, then I will give you thirty sheets and thirty change of garments: . . .

'And he said unto them, Out of the eater came forth meat, and out of the strong came forth sweetness. And they could not in three days expound the riddle' (verses 10–12, 14).

See 1194–1200.

383. TIMNA. See note to 219.

384. *highth*. Milton's spelling of 'highth' must be kept, as it indicates his pronunciation.

389. For the bribe in question see Judges xvi. 5.

394. *My capital secret*: a play upon the root sense (Latin, *caput*, 'head') and the derived sense of 'chief, supreme'. Cf. *P.L.* xii. 383.

402. *must'ring*. The next few lines contain a cluster of military metaphors for Dalila's treatment of her victim (see also 236).

403. *blandish'd parleys*. 'Blandish' (Latin, *blandus*, 'soft, caressing') was common in Middle English, and remained current until the seventeenth century, after which it became literary or jocular.

404. *surceased*. Compare:

> The great Arch-Angel from his warlike toile
> Surceas'd,
>
> > (*P.L.* vi. 258).

422. *Divine impulsion prompting*. This reference to Samson's earlier inspirations helps, like others (221–4, 526, 638), to prepare for the special inspiration which leads to the catastrophe. See 1381–9.

424. *I state not that*. There seems no precise parallel to this use of 'state', perhaps suggested to Milton by such expressions as 'to state a case' for discussion. Together with several other unique phrases in this poem (see 373, 551, 803), it shows how Milton achieves a consistently unusual quality in his diction.

434. *a popular Feast*. See 16 n. 'Then the lords of the Philistines gathered them together for to offer a great sacrifice unto Dagon their God, and to rejoice: for they said, Our god hath delivered Samson our enemy into our hand' (Judges xvi. 23).

438–9. The unusual word-order gives emphasis.

439. *who slew'st them many a slain*. 'The "them" is a sort of dative of reference . . . and is very common in Greek and in French; it cannot be translated, but must be paraphrased' (Churton Collins). The sense here would be: 'whom they had seen slay so many of them.' See also 537–8.

453. Compare:

> How wilt thou reason with them, how refute
> Their Idolisms, Traditions, Paradoxes?
>
> (*P.R.* iv. 234).

463. *enter lists with.* See 1087 n.

471. *blank.* Compare *Hamlet*, III. ii:

> Each opposite that blanks the face of joy.

See also *P.L.* ix. 890 and *Comus*, 452.

473. *I as a Prophecy receive.* 'The receiving of words said as an omen was a common custom among the Greeks' (Churton Collins). Prophecies, or hints of prophecy, in drama are a common means of pointing forward, and inducing expectation.

495. *blab.* Cf. Chaucer, *Troylus*, iii. 299:

> Proverbis canst thi self ynow, and wost
> Ayenst that vice for to bene a blabbe.

499–501. 'The Greek myths meant are such as that of Tantalus, condemned to Hell for divulging heavenly secrets' (Masson). There are various versions of the story of King Tantalus, but all agree that severe punishment was inflicted on him in Hell. The commonest explanation is that Zeus, having invited Tantalus to a banquet, spoke to him in confidence of certain secrets, which Tantalus later revealed.

515. *God offended.* For the idiom see 165 n.

528. *The Sons of* ANAK: the Anakim, a race of giants supposed to dwell anciently at Hebron (see 148). They were conquered by Joshua and Caleb in their wars against the Canaanite peoples (Joshua xiv. 12–15).

blazed. In many contexts the sense of 'trumpeting' is fused with that of a bright fire or flame, as in *Julius Caesar*, II. ii:

> The heavens themselves blaze forth the death of princes.

531. *my affront*: a meeting with me face to face, confronting me. Cf. *P.L.* i. 391.

533. *venereal trains.* 'Venereal' is from the Latin *venereus*, 'pertaining to Venus', the goddess of love. 'Trains' means actions which *draw* somebody *on*.

537. *who shore me.* See 439 n.

538. *Wether*: often used depreciatingly, as in:

>I am a tainted wether of the flock,
>Meetest for death:
>>(*Merchant of Venice*, IV. i. 114).

543. *the dancing Ruby.* Cf. *P.L.* v. 633. This and the following lines refer to Samson's vows of abstinence as a Nazarite. See 30–32 n.

545. 'And the vine said unto them, Should I leave my wine, which cheereth God and man, and go to be promoted over the trees?' (Judges ix. 13).

548. *Against the Eastern ray.* Merritt Hughes points out that it was an ancient belief that the most wholesome water rose from a spring in the face of the rising sun. A closely parallel passage to this is quoted by Thyer from Tasso, *Il Mondo Creato*, Giornata Terza, 135 et seq.

549. *Heav'n's fiery rod.* See *P.L.* iii. 583–6.

550. *the clear milky juice.* Compare:

>nectarous draughts between, from milkie stream,
>Berrie or grape:
>>>(*P.L.* v. 306).

557. *liquid.* The Latin *liquidus*, 'flowing', was also used in poetry to mean 'clear'. Cf. *The Faerie Queene*, III. iv. 49:

>And with her pineons cleaves the liquid firmament.

571. *craze.* Compare:

>God looking forth will trouble all his Host
>And craze thir Chariot wheels:
>>(*P.L.* xii. 210).

574. *draff.* Cf. Chaucer, *Prologue to Parson's Tale*:

>Why shuld I sowen draff out of my fist
>When I may sowen wheat if that me liste?

See also *P.L.* x. 630.

581–3. See Judges xv. 18–19: one interpretation of this passage was that God caused a hollow space to be cloven in a piece of ground, or rock, called *Lehi*, 'the jaw'.

586. This passage is yet another of those premonitions which point forward to the end of the play (see 473 n.); it is also charged with tragic irony, since the outcome is far from what Manoa had in mind.

594. *genial spirits*. In classical pagan belief every person at birth was allotted an attendant spirit called in Latin a *genius*, which determined his character, guided his fortunes, and finally led him out of the world. Milton's use of 'genial' carries some of these associations. 'Genial spirits' here suggests the most deeply seated energies or volitions which sustain the individual life—the 'will to live'.

600. *humours black*. Our word 'melancholy' means literally 'black humour' or 'black bile', deriving from the medieval and Renaissance theory of physiology. This accounted for the various states of men's minds and bodies, in health and sickness, by the action in them of four 'humours' (blood, choler, phlegm, bile), which were present in all constitutions in varying proportions.

605. *healing words*: see 184–6 and n. The expression occurs also in *P.L.* ix. 290. Here it anticipates the metaphors of mental wounds and diseases with which Samson opens his next speech.

Lines 606–51

Throughout the poem, when emotion is intensified the verse passes from blank verse to lyric. So Samson, when Manoa leaves him, expresses in a monody his mental torment and his loss of all worldly hope. He has already referred to the thoughts which torture him (19–22, 330, 458–9). Manoa's visit and conversation, perhaps by making his situation more vivid to him, have produced an overwhelming despondency.

612. *accidents*: regularly used for the symptoms or phases of an illness, especially if unfavourable. Compare: 'There began . . . a disease then new: which of the accidents and manner thereof they called the Sweating-sicknesse' (Bacon, *Henry VII*, 9).

614. *entrails*. Perhaps here 'the flesh', like the Latin *viscera* (Churton Collins).

624. *my apprehensive tenderest parts*. Milton means those organs or faculties which receive sensuous or mental impressions.

627. *med'cinal.* Compare:

> And yet more med'cinal is it then that *Moly*
> That *Hermes* once to wise *Ulysses* gave:
>> (*Comus*, 636).

Pronounce 'med'c'nal', the last two syllables being elided.

628. ALP: used to mean any high mountain, as in Italian verse. Compare:

> O're many a frozen, many a Fierie Alpe,
>> (*P.L.* ii. 620).

630. *benumbing Opium.* Opium (Latin, *opium*, Greek, ὄπιον, 'poppy-juice') was mainly used as a narcotic or sedative.

635. *message.* Cf. Chaucer, *Man of Law's Tale*, 235:

> The hooly lawes of oure Alkaron,
> Yeven by Goddes message Makomete.

twice descending. See 24 and 361.

637. *amain.* See 1304.

639. *nerve.* See also 1646.

Lines 652–709

Feeling the depth of Samson's despair, the Chorus remarks on the vanity of attempting to console such pain by means of moral reflections. Only God can sustain the dejected spirit (652–66). They ask why God should deal so arbitrarily with human beings: other creatures, below and above man in the scale of creation, are less subject to changes of fortune (667–73). And it is not only common and insignificant people who so suffer, but those whom God has apparently chosen and favoured as his servants (674–86). The ultimate fate of these elect beings is often as wretched as if they had deserved no better than the rest (687–704). The Chorus prays that Samson may not end in his present misery; let peace at least come to him in his misfortunes (705–9).

661. *seems a tune.* Churton Collins quotes Ecclesiasticus xxii. 6: 'A tale out of season is as music in mourning.'

662. *mood.* The term comes from the four 'moods' i.e. modes or measures of Greek music, the Dorian, the Ionian, the Phrygian, and

the Lydian, which are often referred to by Milton (see *P.L.* i. 550 and *L'Allegro*, 136).

667. 'What is man, that thou art mindful of him?' (Psalm viii. 4). See also Job vii. 17.

670. *Temper'st.* Cf. Spenser, *Mother Hubberds Tale*, 1292–4:

> his snakie wand,
> With which the damned ghosts he gouerneth,
> And furies rules, and Tartare tempereth.

672. *The Angelic orders*. Early Christian and earlier Jewish tradition provided the basis for the conception of the angelic hierarchies, fully developed in the Middle Ages and surviving in *Paradise Lost*

677. *Heads without name*. ' "Heads" is a common synonym in Greek and Latin for "persons" ' (Churton Collins, who cites Livy's *ignota capita*).

683. *highth.* See 384 n.

691. *trespass or omission.* Sins or faults can be of two kinds, either acts committed against the moral law or omissions to fulfil it.

695–702. 'There has been an occult reference all through this chorus to the wreck of the Puritan cause by the Restoration; but in these lines the reference becomes distinct. Milton has the trials of Vane and the Regicides in his mind. He himself had been in danger of the law; and though he had escaped, it was to a "crude (premature) old age", afflicted by painful diseases, from which his temperate life might have been expected to exempt him' (Masson).

The Parliament that recalled Charles II from exile in 1660 proceeded at once to the trial and punishment of all who had taken part in the condemnation and execution of his father in 1649. A full account of the trials and sentences is given in Masson's *Life of John Milton*, vol. vi, book i, chap. 1, pp. 76–98. Several of the Regicides, including the chief offenders, Cromwell, Ireton, Bradshaw, and Pride, were dead. In December 1660 Parliament ordered that the bodies of these four should be disinterred, 'dragged to Tyburn, there to hang for some time, and afterwards be buried under the gallows' (p. 113). On 30 January, the anniversary of the death of

Charles I, this order was carried out. A contemporary newspaper account is quoted by Masson: 'This day, Jan. 30 . . . was doubly observed, not only by a solemn fast, sermons, and prayers, in every parish church, for the precious blood of our late pious sovereign King Charles the First, of ever glorious memory, but also by publicly dragging those odious carcases of Oliver Cromwell, Henry Ireton, and John Bradshaw, to Tyburn. . . . All the way . . . the universal outcry and curses of the people went along with them. When the three carcases were at Tyburn, they were pulled out of their coffins, and hanged at the several angles of that triple tree, where they hung till the sun was set; after which they were taken down, and their heads cut off, and their loathsome trunks thrown into a deep hole under the gallows' (p. 123). The heads of Cromwell, Bradshaw, and Ireton were placed on poles on the top of Westminster Hall, where they remained for several years.

The new Parliament which met in 1661 proceeded to the trial of Sir Henry Vane and Colonel Lambert, who were not among the Regicides. Vane was executed at Tower Hill in June 1662.

701. *Though not disordinate.* Milton in his later years suffered painfully from gout, which in his case was certainly not due to earlier intemperance. He is described at this time as 'pale but not cadaverous, his hands and fingers gouty and with chalkstones. Among other discourse he expressed himself to this purpose: that, was he free from the pain this gave him, his blindness would be tolerable' (Masson, *Life*, vol. vi, p. 679). Milton's blindness, total after 1652, may also have been connected with the gout which afflicted him later.

Lines 710–1009

The Chorus sees Dalila approaching, opulently dressed and attended by Philistine maidens; her stately bearing is described with some irony (710–24). Even at the mention of her approach, Samson expresses his revulsion (715). She hesitates, apparently moved at the sight of his wretched state (726–31); and at last addresses him in a conciliating manner, acknowledging her past fault, professing repentance and a wish to make him some amends (732–47). Samson violently denounces these advances as mere hypocrisy (748–65). But she continues to plead: she acted through weakness, but he also was weak, and his weakness should make him forgive hers (773–89). Moreover, she was moved by love: she wished to keep him by her, and did not believe the Philistines intended to do more than keep him captive (790–810). Samson rejects her plea: he will not condone his own weakness, why should he condone hers (823–35)? And what genuine love would seek fulfilment through treachery? Such arguments only reveal the wickedness they try to hide (836–42). Dalila then shifts her ground: her judgement was swayed, she says, by the insistence of the Philistine priests and rulers, arguing in the name of patriotism and religion (843–70). Samson replies that, once she was his wife, she owed no further allegiance to her own people; only false religion would seek to be advanced by crime, and the Gods of the Philistines are therefore self-condemned (876–900). Dalila takes refuge in querulousness, which is met with sarcasm (901–4). She then resorts to more material inducements, suggesting the comfort and affection she may offer him, if she can obtain his release (907–17). But Samson is no longer susceptible to such temptations, especially since he could now expect less good faith, if possible, than before: his blindness would put him at her mercy. He prefers his prison to her house (928–50). Dalila makes a last effort to prevail, by arousing his senses (951). The ferocity of his reaction convinces her that her cause is hopeless, and at last she reveals her true self: why should she humble herself further (960–8)? For her ill fame in Israel, she will be recompensed by the gratitude and esteem of the Philistines, who will treat her as a national heroine (975–90). Henceforth she will accept their homage, and leave Samson to his fate (991–6). This parting revelation of her true nature is well understood by Samson and the Chorus (997–1002). The Chorus is impressed by Samson's inflexibility in the face of temptation (1003–7).

The encounter of Samson and Dalila is the greatest dramatic opportunity which Milton's 'fable' offers him: he makes it the centre of his play and the turning-point in his hero's fluctuating state of mind. Dalila's appearance has been prepared for by repeated references to her fatal influence (200-2, 229–30, 392–419); it is essential that Samson's repudiation of her should be put to the test. She thus contributes the highest dramatic interest in the plot; and she also contributes a valuable poetic enrichment. For the general atmosphere of *Samson Agonistes* is stern and dark: Dalila's feminine softness and elegance provide a welcome and effective contrast. Moreover, her stubborn cunning, however detestable, is in effective contrast to the emphatic uprightness of most of the other characters. Her part is indeed next to that of Samson in completeness of realization: she is convincingly feminine, and convincingly evil.

The effect of this scene on Samson is decisive. While Manoa's intervention, holding out a possibility of some material relief, leaves Samson utterly dejected, Dalila's temptations, which he rejects in favour of his present misery, rouse him from his lethargy. The moral strength with which he resists her is the same strength with which he has submitted to his punishment; and from what seems a negative decision springs a positive energy. Samson's moral regeneration began, we are to assume, even before the beginning of the play; but it is the scene with Dalila which makes its nature clear. Repentance and acceptance of punishment are not negative but positive decisions: they may involve outward passivity, but they are inwardly active and invigorating.

715. TARSUS. Ships of Tarshish are often mentioned in the Old Testament (see Psalm xlviii. 7; Isaiah xxiii. 1 and 14); but Tarshish is usually identified with *Tartessus* in southern Spain, not, as here, with *Tarsus* the capital of Cilicia. In any case Milton wishes to avoid the harsh 'sh' sounds in *Tarshish*.

716. JAVAN. Noah's grandson, Javan or Ion, fourth son of Japhet, was supposed to have peopled Greece with his descendants (see *P.L.* i. 508). Milton wishes to indicate the eastern Mediterranean as a whole.

GADIER: a Phoenician city, Gadera in Greek, Gades in Latin; it is now Cadiz, and is here used as representative of the western Mediterranean. Compare:

> From *Gallia*, *Gades*, and the *Brittish* West,
> (*P.R.* iv. 77).

717. *bravery*. Compare the modern naval expression 'dressed overall'.

720. *Amber scent*. This is a solid fatty substance of grey or blackish colour, with a sweet earthy smell. It is produced in the intestines of the spermaceti whale, and found floating in the sea or washed up on shore. In Europe it is used now only in the preparation of

perfumes, but it is still used in the East in cooking and medicine. Compare:

> Beasts of chase, or fowl of game,
> In pastry built, or from the spit, or boiled,
> Gris-amber-steamed;
>
> (*P.R.* ii. 342–4).

748. HYAENA. A marginal note to 'hyena' in Ecclesiasticus xiii. 19 in the Geneva Bible of 1560 says: 'Which is a wilde beaste that counterfaiteth the voyce of men, and so entiseth them out of their houses and devoureth them.'

763. *bosom snake*. 'To cherish a viper in one's bosom' was a proverbial phrase. Cf. *Richard II*, III. ii. 131:

> Snakes, in my heart-blood warm'd, that sting my heart!

775. *importune*: formerly an alternative form of 'importunate' (Italian, *importuno*). As in *P.R.* ii. 404, pronounce:

> Curiósity, inquísitive, impórtune.

(But in *P.L.* ix. 610, the stress is on the last syllable.)

785. *parle*. Cf. *Hamlet*, I. i. 62–63:

> So frown'd he once, when in an angry parle,
> He smote the sledded Polacks on the ice.

795. See note to 219.

803. *That made for me*. To 'make for' meant to 'work in favour of', to 'help', someone or something. But perhaps Dalila means here, 'That (argument) weighed heavily with me'. See note to 424.

829. *Weakness is thy excuse*. Samson is recalling Dalila's arguments and rebutting them one by one. See 836, and 1192–1219.

843. *determin'st*. Two meanings of the word seem to be combined: (i) 'determine' as 'bring to an end'; and (ii) 'determine' as 'decide'. The sense would be either, 'Since you bring to a close my plea of weakness as being no plea'; or, 'since you decide that weakness can be no plea'; or both.

857–61. The Old Testament makes no mention of priestly influence on Dalila; Milton is colouring the story with his own anticlerical convictions.

866. *rife*. Compare:

> whereof so rife
> There went a fame in Heav'n
>   (*P.L.* i. 650).

885–6. See Genesis ii. 24.

895. *But zeal moved thee*. See notes to 829 and 836.

901. *varnish'd colours*. Both 'colours' and 'varnish' are frequent metaphors for deceit. Cf. *The Tempest*, I. ii. 143:

> With colours fairer painted their foul ends.

906. *peals*. See 235.

920. *I to the Lords will intercede*: 'I will go *to* the lords and intercede *with* them.' 'With' is the correct preposition with 'intercede'. Milton has used 'to' because he has in mind the idiom 'I will to the lords' (see 1250).

932. *trains*. See note to 533.

933. *toils*. Cf. *Antony and Cleopatra*, v. ii. 347–9:

> she looks like sleep,
> As she would catch another Antony
> In her strong toil of grace.

934. The Greek myths of the enchantress Circe, and of the Sirens, are suggested by these images of a magic potion and of spells sung to music. Cf. *Comus*, 50–53:

> who knows not *Circe*,
> The daughter of the Sun? whose charmed Cup
> Whoever tasted, lost his upright shape,
> And downward fell into a groveling Swine?

936. *Adder's wisdom*. The supposed deafness of the adder was proverbial in the Middle Ages, as a result of Psalm lviii. 4, 5: 'They are like the deaf adder, that stoppeth her ear; which will not hearken to the voice of the charmers, charming never so wisely.' But this passage refers in fact to an exceptional individual, a wilfully deaf adder, which is not, like the rest of the species, amenable to music.

944. *insult*. See 113.

945. *uxorious*. Compare: 'Effeminate and uxorious Magistrates,

govern'd and overswaid at home under a Feminine usurpation'
(Milton, *Eikonoclastes*, 64).

946. *perfet*. Milton's spelling represents the old pronunciation.
See 324 n.

967. *evil omen*. Dalila so refers to Samson's bitter farewell, and his
irony at the expense of her future reputation (see 954–9).

971–4. This allegory of Fame is of a kind often found in classical
poets and orators, as well as in medieval and Renaissance literature,
but its details are Milton's own. In Chaucer's *House of Fame*, the
Goddess Fame makes use of two trumpets: one black, for Infamy or
Slander, the other golden, for praise. These might have suggested
Milton's 'contrary blast', though this seems to come from two mouths
rather than two trumpets. Moreover, Milton's Fame is a God, not
a Goddess, and the contrast of colours in Chaucer's trumpets belongs
here to the God's wings, on which he carries names and reputations
throughout the world.

973–4. The rhymed couplet gives the effect of a proverb. Such
gnomic or sententious couplets were often used by Elizabethan
dramatists.

976. The tribe of Dan, to which Samson belonged, had its territory
next to that of the tribe of Judah.

981. *In* ECRON, GAZA, ASDOD, *and in* GATH: four of the five chief
cities of the Philistines. Cf. *P.L.* i. 465–6:

> in *Gath* and *Ascalon*
> And *Accaron* and *Gaza*'s frontier bounds.

982. *famousest*. Milton is fond of this type of superlative.

988–90. Jael's betrayal of the fugitive Canaanite leader is related
in Judges iv. 17–22. She is 'renown'd in Mount Ephraim' because
Deborah made a song in her praise (Judges v), and Deborah 'dwelt
under the palm tree of Deborah between Ramah and Bethel in
Mount Ephraim' (Judges iv. 5).

993. *piety*: devotion to duty; especially, in Latin, devotion to one's
own people and country.

1003–5. Cf. *P.L.* x. 937–46.

1008. *Love-quarrels oft in pleasing concord end.* Cf. Terence, *Andria*, III. iii. 23:

Amantium irae amoris integratio est.

The line was translated by Richard Edwards in *A Paradise of Dainty Devices* (1576) as the refrain of a song:

The falling out of faithful friends is the renewing of love.

Lines 1010–60

The Chorus moralizes on the incomprehensible nature of women's love, and of women. If women's love could be won and kept by physical advantages or by moral virtues, Samson's two wives would not have treated him as they did (1010–24). Can the explanation be that woman was endowed with so much outward beauty that her inward equipment, her mind and moral sense, was left incomplete (1025–30)? Or is the feminine disposition too self-regarding to be capable of true love, or at least of constancy (1031)? Whatever the explanation, women deceive men's hopes: after marriage many wise and good men find the wife of their choice a hindrance and not a helpmate (1034–45). The good wife, who smoothes her husband's way to virtue, is rare. However, God has more esteem for virtue won in the face of difficulties (1046–52). We must conclude that God rightly gave men authority over women, and that he means them to use it; for the dominance of women is disastrous (1053–60).

1014. *hit*: suggests the uncertainty of any conclusion, as in 'to hit upon' an idea.

1016. *Much like thy riddle.* See 382–7 n.

1018. TIMNIAN. See 219 n.

1020. *Paranymph*: from a Greek word meaning 'friend of the bridegroom'. See Judges xiv. 20.

1038. *Intestine.* Its most common use is with reference to human or animal bodies, but this by a metaphor is extended to mean 'domestic' or 'civil'. Pronounce 'intestin'. Here it suggests the metaphor of civil war.

1039. *A cleaving mischief.* This phrase for a disloyal or troublesome wife has been thought to refer to the poisoned shirt sent to Hercules by his wife Deianeira, which 'cleaved' to his body and caused his death (Masson, followed by Merritt Hughes). But the allusion, if it is present, is very obscurely given. 'Cleaving' may be used in its other sense of 'dividing' or 'penetrating', and the expression would then continue the metaphor of 'the thorn in the flesh', which Milton has just used (1037–8).

1034–45. Compare Adam's outburst against women in *P.L.* x. 888–99. Merritt Hughes relates both passages to the invective against women in the Hippolytus of Euripides, ll. 616–17. But Milton's eloquence may have also a more personal inspiration.

1046–8. Compare the praise of a good wife in Proverbs xxi. 10–28:

'Who can find a virtuous woman? for her price is far above rubies. The heart of her husband doth safely trust in her. . . . She will do him good and not evil all the days of her life. . . .'

1060. *female usurpation*. Milton had quoted St. Paul in *The Doctrine and Discipline of Divorce*, II. xv: 'But I suffer not a woman to teach, nor to usurp authority over the man, but to be in silence' (1 Timothy ii. 12). See 945 n.

Lines 1061–1267

The Chorus observes the approach of Harapha, a gigantic and seemingly quarrelsome Philistine (1065–73). Harapha announces that he has come to see with his own eyes the famous Hebrew champion, and to estimate his strength for himself; he professes to be sorry that they never met in the days of Samson's prowess, when he, Harapha, would surely have come off victorious (1075–1113). Samson offers to make good the omission at any time: were the encounter to take place in a confined space, himself armed only with a stick would overthrow Harapha fully armed (1104–29). Only magic could bring him such a victory, replies Harapha; but Samson declares he owns no magic but his strength, the gift of God. Let then Harapha as the champion of Dagon meet him as the champion of the God of Israel—for God will accept him once more as his champion, now that he is penitent (1130–77). Harapha evades the challenge by sneering at Samson as a criminal. Samson rebuts his accusations, and repeats the challenge (1178–1223). But it is plain that Harapha will not undertake the trial of strength, though he blusters and threatens

(1224–6, 1230–2, 1242–3). He departs with the intention, as the Chorus fears, of complaining to the Philistine lords of Samson's insolence (1250–2). But Samson has been thoroughly roused by the encounter (1227–30, 1237–41, 1247–9); and he makes light of any possible danger to himself (1253–61). Increased ill treatment can only at the worst bring him release by death, and it may well also bring disaster on his oppressors (1262–7).

The battle of words with Harapha is no mere interlude, though it may seem to touch on no practical issue of any importance. It provides a certain relaxation after the emotional and moral tension of the scene with Dalila; there is sardonic comedy as the Philistine champion betrays the emptiness of his boasting, and Samson insults him more and more freely. But the true dramatic function of the scene is to display the change which has taken place in Samson since Manoa left him. Then he had seen himself as superseded, of no further account in the contest between the God of Israel and Dagon. Now he finds, as the scene proceeds, that he can yet be, that he still is and must continue to be, God's servant and champion. He hints at a possible revenge upon his enemies (1265–7); but the most significant fact is his renewed desire for action.

1062. *contracted.* We still speak of 'contracting' debts or an illness.

1064. *my riddling days.* See 382–7 n.

1068. HARAPHA. The name comes from 2 Samuel xxi. 16, 17 where certain Philistine champions are called the sons of Raph of Harapha. The Authorized Version translates the words as 'the sons of the giant'.

1080. OG: King of Bashan at the time of the wanderings of the Israelites in the wilderness. He was 'of the remnant of the giants' (Joshua xiii. 12). The conquest of Og by Moses was held to be one of the great events of Jewish history.

ANAK. See 528 n.

EMIMS: a giant race of Moab (double plural from Emim). See Deuteronomy ii. 10–11, and Genesis xiv. 5.

1081–2. Compare:

> Not to know mee argues your selves unknown
>
> (*P.L.* iv. 830).

1081. KIRIATHAIM: a town in Moab.

1093. *Gyves.* Compare:

> his stockings foul'd,
> Ungarter'd, and down-gyvéd to his ancle;
> > (*Hamlet*, II. i. 79–80).

1109. *assassinated.* This use of the word is obsolete. 'Assassin' and its derivatives go back to an Arabic word meaning 'hashish-eater'. It was first applied, in the sense of a treacherous or secret murderer, to the followers of 'the Old Man of the Mountains', a Persian sect of Moslems. They employed murder as a political weapon, and prepared themselves for it by means of the drug.

1112. *chamber Ambushes*: i.e. when the victim feels secure as being at home or in a friendly house, and is at a further disadvantage because of the confined space.

1120. *Brigandine*: a coat of armour suitable for a 'brigand' in the original sense of the word, i.e. 'a light-armed, irregular foot-soldier'.

1122. *A Weaver's beam*: like that of Goliath: 'the staff of his spear was like a weaver's beam' (1 Samuel xvii. 7).

seven-times-folded shield. Milton wishes to recall two such shields described by Homer and Virgil: the shield of Ajax, made of seven layers of bull's hide (*Iliad* vii. 220), and the seven-fold shield of Turnus which was pierced by Aeneas (*Aeneid* xii. 925).

1132–4. Enchanted weapons are common in medieval tales of chivalry, and appear in Ariosto and Spenser.

arm'd thee or charm'd thee strong. For this type of jingle see 301 n.

1138. *chafed.* See 1246.

ruffled Porcupines. Cf. *Hamlet*, I. v. 19–20:

> And each particular hair to stand an end,
> Like quills upon the fretful porpentine.

1139–44. In medieval trials by arms the champions first took the following oath: 'I do swear that I have not upon me, nor upon any of the arms I shall use, words, charms, or enchantments, to which I trust for help to conquer my enemy, but that I do only trust in God, in my right, and in the strength of my body and arms' (Todd).

1164. *boist'rous.* There is a sarcastic allusion to Samson's hair as the seat of his strength.

1168. *for such they are From thine*. Samson's ill treatment, though deserved, is unjustly inflicted by the Philistines.

1184. *deliver'd bound*. See Judges xv. 9–15, and 258 n.

1185–8. After his betrayal by the woman of Timnath, Samson paid his wager to the Philistines by the following means:

'And the Spirit of the LORD came upon him, and he went down to Ashkelon, and slew thirty men of them, and took their spoil, and gave change of garments unto them which expounded the riddle' (Judges xiv. 19). See 382–7 n.

1192–3. This seems a somewhat disingenuous argument, since Samson's justification for marrying the woman of Timnath was that he would thus have opportunities to molest the Philistines. See 222–6, and Judges xiv. 4.

1194–1200. For the wedding at Timnath and the riddle see 382–7.

1195. *Politician*. The word had a bad sense in Elizabethan English and for the greater part of the seventeenth century. Cf. *1 Henry IV*, I. iii. 239–41:

Why, look you, I am whipp'd and scourg'd with rods,
Nettled, and stung with pismires, when I hear
Of this vile politician, Bolingbroke.

1197. Milton takes from Josephus (*Antiquities*, v. viii. 6) the idea that Samson's thirty wedding-companions were spies set by the Philistines.

1218. *my known offence*. The 'offence' is Samson's betrayal of his secret to Dalila; it is 'known' because she informed the Philistines. But one is tempted to adopt Sampson's conjecture, 'mine own offence'.

1222. *thrice*. It was customary to repeat a formal challenge three times.

1224. *enroll'd*: named on a list, as a conscript or one of a gang of labourers. Criminals and persons in menial positions were not allowed to have recourse to trial by arms, which was the privilege of nobles and fighting men.

1228. *descant*. In musical terminology a descant is a varied accompaniment to a simple theme: hence this meaning of an amplification or commentary on a given subject. Compare:

> Why, I, in this weak piping time of peace,
> Have no delight to pass away the time,
> Unless to see my shadow in the sun
> And descant on mine own deformity:
> > (*Richard III*, I. i. 24–27).

verdit. See 324 n.

1231. BAAL-ZEBUB: the name under which Baal was worshipped by the Philistines at Ecron. See 1242, and *P.L.* i. 81, 271 and ii. 299, 378. These oaths by Philistine deities are a conventional device to lend some 'local colour' to the character of Harapha.

1238. *bulk without spirit vast.* 'Without spirit' is used adverbially, and is best spoken rapidly, as if hyphenated.

1242. ASTAROTH: or Ashtoreth, the principal goddess of the Sidonians, and worshipped among the Phoenicians generally. She seems to have been pre-eminently the deity of sexual passion. See I Kings xi. 5 and 33.

1244. *crestfall'n*: with drooping crest. The expression implies that too great a confidence has gone before.

1246. *chafe.* See 1138.

1248–9. 2 Samuel xxi tells of a giant in Gath who had four sons who 'fell by the hand of David, and by the hand of his servants' (verse 22). In Hebrew this giant is called simply 'Rapha'. It is not clear in this chapter (verse 19), or in I Samuel xvii, that Goliath was a son of this giant, though he was 'of Gath'.

1250. *He will directly to the Lords.* This omission of the verb of motion is common in Elizabethan English.

1253. *offer'd fight.* See 165 n.

Lines 1268–96

The Chorus has also been invigorated by Harapha's visit: it exults in the splendour of heroic action against the enemies of God and freedom (1268–86). Heroic patience under suffering is also, of course, a means of sanctification (1287–91). Samson still has the strength to

do great deeds, but in view of his blindness, the Chorus is inclined
to foresee for him only the spiritual triumph of patience (1292–6).

1278. *feats of War defeats*. Note the play on words, and compare
301 and 1134.

1281. *Magazines*. The word goes back to an Arabic word for
'storehouse'.

1294. *sight bereaved*. See 165 n.

Lines 1297–1440

The Chorus sees a Philistine official approaching, and anticipates
further trouble for Samson (1297–1307). The officer delivers his
message: Samson is commanded to appear before the Philistine lords
and people, assembled for Dagon's festival, and to entertain them
with feats of strength (1308–18). Samson emphatically refuses: his
religion forbids him to take part in heathen rites, and besides, he will
not abase himself by using his strength to amuse his oppressors
(1319–42). The officer warns him that this refusal will probably
bring down wrath upon him, and returns with it to those who sent
him (1333 and 1345). Left alone with the Chorus, Samson justifies
his refusal: God would be insulted by acceptance, though no doubt
God might grant a special dispensation for a special purpose, in such
circumstances (1377–9). As he says this Samson is evidently struck
by some new thought, for he at once reverses his decision, informing
the Chorus that he will in fact obey the Philistines' commands,
though not in such a way as to disgrace his religion (1381–9). The
Philistine official returns, charged with threats; but Samson agrees
to go with him, and departs, taking farewell of the Chorus, and once
more assuring them that he will do nothing unworthy (1390–1426).
The Chorus blesses him as he goes, invoking some special manifesta-
tion of the Holy Spirit on his behalf (1427–40).

With the message from the Philistine lords the action enters its
last phase: there is a quickening of pace which goes with immediate
decisions and their consequences. The hero's state of mind has
undergone its evolution, and he is now ready for whatever right
action may present itself. This completed dramatic creation is also
a completed poetic symbol, capable of carrying the final weight of
meaning Milton has in store.

The scene of Samson's decision and departure is made interesting chiefly by Milton's insistence on its theological implications. Samson emphasizes the religious obstacles to what he then decides to do. Milton indicates that his decision is made by an impulse sent from God (1381–1389). Only some such view could justify Samson's last deed, involving self-destruction. (In this connexion Merritt Hughes quotes from Donne's *Biathanatos*, III. v, a passage which argues that Samson's action can scarcely be distinguished from suicide.) In the event the Chorus recognizes that Samson has been inspired by God (1689); and they assume now that he may be moved by the spirit of God, as he has been before (1427–40). And Samson has several times referred to his consciousness of having been inspired (221–4, 526, 638), and to his sense that he has since lost this communication with God (632).

1303. *quaint*. The original sense is 'cunning, skilled'. See *The Faerie Queene*, IV. x. 22.

1308. EBREWS. Milton frequently, though not uniformly, uses this spelling (Italian *ebreo*). See also 1319 and 1540.

1317. *hearten'd*. O.E.D. quotes: 'Good Ale, which inwardly must hearten him' (1586).

1346. *stoutness*. Compare:

> Sir, his stoutness
> When he did stand for consul, which he lost
> By lack of stooping,—
>
> (*Coriolanus*, V. v. 27–29).

1349. *highth*. See 384 n.

1362. *unclean*. See 321 and n.

1375. *in his jealousy*. See Exodus xx. 3–5: 'Thou shalt have no other gods before me . . . for I the LORD thy God am a jealous God. . . .'

1396. *Engines*: from Greek μηχαναί. It is not certain that 'machines' are meant. See *P.L.* i. 749.

1418. *Lords are Lordliest in their wine*. Milton may be alluding to the drunken arrogance not infrequently shown by the nobility of the Restoration period.

1419. *well-feasted Priest*. References to clerics as bloated with food are common, perhaps too common, in Milton's anti-episcopal prose works.

1433. *after his message told*. See 23–29 n. and 165 n.

1436. *In the camp of* DAN. The words come from the Authorized Version. See 131 n.

Lines 1441–1659

Manoa returns, to report to the Chorus concerning his son's ransom: he has been given grounds for hope during his visits to various Philistine notabilities (1441–1507). A placid and hopeful conversation with the Chorus is interrupted, first by a shout which indicates that the assembled Philistines are welcoming Samson's appearance (1472–5), and finally by an appalling outcry (1508–14), which leaves Manoa and the Chorus terrified and bewildered, yet half hoping that some great disaster has overtaken their enemies (1521–33). A fellow Israelite then arrives, who gives them the chief facts at first (1558–70, 1582–9), and then describes more fully what has happened (1596–1659), reporting Samson's last words (1640–5).

The methods of this final scene are thoroughly Greek, in their presentation of the matter with most effect. Dramatic irony gives a heightened interest to Manoa's talk with the Chorus; the comments of the Chorus have a gnomic concision. The Messenger discharges his task according to precedent, at first briefly, then at length. These devices are not only efficient in themselves; they also illustrate that for Milton the conscious application of literary conventions is in itself a source of beauty and interest.

1445. *Peace with you brethren*. This is a frequent greeting in the Old Testament. Compare: 'peace be to thee, peace be to thy house, peace be to all' (1 Samuel xxv. 6).

1461–71. 'The different shades of feeling among the men in power in England after the Restoration may be supposed to be glanced at in this passage—obstinate and revengeful Royalism, strongest among the High Church party; and so on' (Masson).

1479. *richest*. There is no indication in the Book of Judges that Mánoa was a rich man. See the note to the Argument.

1481. *part*. See also 1719. Note the irony of this line: Manoa does not leave without Samson, for he takes Samson's body with him (1725–33).

1497–8. 'Samson's hair is as it were a fort of strength, the single hairs corresponding to single soldiers' (Churton Collins).

1507. *as next*. The Chorus are members of Samson's tribe, the Danites. See 181.

1512. *inhabitation*. According to Churton Collins, 'the inhabited world, ἡ οἰκουμένη'.

1515. *ruin*. Cf. *P.L.* i. 46.

1519. *dismal*. This word originally meant the 'evil days' (Latin, *dies mali*) of the medieval calendar. These were twenty-four specific days of the year which were supposed to be unlucky. The word came to be used as an adjective, referring sometimes to days, but also with a wider application. Milton often uses the word with its astrological associations of 'fatal, disastrous', as in:

> I, when no other durst, sole undertook
> The dismal expedition to find out
> And ruin Adam,
>
> (*P.R.* i. 101).

See also *P.L.* ii. 572. The subsequent loss of these special associations has an unfortunate effect in such passages as:

> The dismal situation waste and wilde,
> (*P.L.* i. 60).

1519–20. Note the rhymed couplets here and in 1525–6. They convey the excitement of the moment.

1529. *dole*. Milton plays on the two meanings of the word: (i) a portion dealt out, as Samson deals it here; and (ii) pain or grief (Italian *duolo*, Latin *dolor*).

1538. *rides post, baits*. Bad news travels swiftly, good news slowly. 'To ride post' was to ride by relays of horses from inn to inn, hence 'posthaste', as quickly as possible. 'To bait' was to make a stay on one's journey to refresh oneself and one's horses, hence to travel at leisure.

1574. *conceived*: imagined. But there is a play upon 'conception' in the sense of 'gestation', as the metaphors of birth and abortion show (1575–6). Editors quote *Love's Labour's Lost*, i. i. 100–1:

> Like an envious sneaping frost,
> That bites the first-born infants of the spring.

1605–10. 'Conceive the building as follows: There is a large semi-circular *covered* space or amphitheatre, filled up with tiers of seats—the roof of which semi-circular building is supported by two great pillars rising from the ground about midpoint of the diameter of the semi-circle. There is no *wall* at this diameter, but only these two pillars; standing near which Samson would look *inside* upon the congregated Philistine lords and others of rank, occupying the tiers of seats under the roof. *Behind* Samson was then an uncovered space where the poorer spectators could stand on any kind of benches under the open sky, seeing Samson's back, and, save where the pillars might interrupt the view, all that went on inside' (Masson).

1608. *sort.* Cf. *Measure for Measure*, IV. iv. 20: 'Give notice to such men of sort and suite as are to meete him.'

1619. *Cataphracts*: from a Greek word meaning 'covered up'. See *P.R.* iii. 311–13.

1621. *Rifted.* Compare:

> to the dread-rattling thunder
> Have I given fire and rifted Jove's stout oak
> With his own bolt:
>
>   (*The Tempest*, v. i. 44–46).

1627. *stupendious.* This was a seventeenth-century form of the word. Cf. *P.L.* x. 350–1:

> Great joy was at thir meeting, and at sight
> Of that stupendious Bridge his joy encreas'd.

1645. *strike all who behold.* Samson's double meaning here recalls Satan's ironic puns in *P.L.* vi. 558–67, when he introduces artillery into the war in Heaven.

1647–8. Earthquakes were supposed to be caused by underground winds or waters seeking to find an outlet. See *P.L.* i. 230–7 and vi. 195–8.

1651–2. The Biblical narrative speaks of many on the roof of the building (Judges xvi. 27); but Milton mentions only deaths caused by the fall of the building on those beneath.

Lines 1660–1758

The Chorus sings of Samson's triumphant death, breaking into semi-choruses to celebrate the defeat of Dagon's worshippers by the true God (1669–86), and the glorious resurrection of Samson's strength (1687–1707). Manoa checks their outburst of grief and praise in a final speech full of pride at his son's glorious death; he dwells on the honours which he and his tribe will bestow on Samson's body (1725–37), and prophesies that a national cult will spring up at his tomb (1738–44). The Chorus concludes with a hymn in praise of Divine Providence. Samson's exploit has vindicated the power and justice of God against doubt and evil: the faithful are left enlightened, their emotions calmed by the tragic greatness they have witnessed (1745–58).

1667–8. 'So the dead which he slew at his death were more than *they* which he slew in his life' (Judges xvi. 30).

1669. The division of the Chorus into two at this point quickens the pace of the verse, both to bring the play to an end, and to correspond to the emotions released.

1671. *regorged.* The prefix 're' in Latin often has an intensive force.

1674. SILO: the Biblical Shiloh. The Ark of the Covenant, the centre of Hebrew worship, was at this time at Shiloh, 'on the north side of Beth-el, on the east side of the highway that goeth up from Beth-el to Shechem, and on the south of Debonah' (Judges xxi. 19). Milton preferred to eliminate the *sh* sound in these Hebrew names; see notes to 138, 715, and 981 (*Asdod* for Ashdod).

his bright Sanctuary. When the tabernacle was set up by Moses: 'Then a cloud covered the tent of the congregation, and the glory of the LORD filled the tabernacle' (Exodus xl. 34).

1675. *he a spirit of frenzy sent.* The idea that 'Quem Deus vult perdere prius dementat' ('Whom God wishes to destroy, he first makes mad') is common in Greek tragic drama. Churton Collins refers to Sophocles, *Antigone*, 621–3.

1685. *to sense reprobate.* 'Reprobate' is 'used especially in metallurgy of an alloy that will not endure the trial, but shows itself to be adulterate when tested' (Skeat). The commonest use of the word is in the religious sense of 'condemned' or 'rejected' by God, and here the religious associations are fully present.

1692–6. Some critics have objected to the comparison of Samson first to 'an evening dragon', and then to an eagle, and have sought to avoid it by suggesting textual error. In fact, as Masson says, 'Milton's meaning is stronger and bolder as the text stands. The blind Samson came among the assembled and seated Philistines like an evening dragon among tame fowl perched on their roosts—i.e. a fearful object, certainly, but on the ground and darkly groping his way; but anon this enemy on the ground is transmuted into an enemy swooping down resistlessly from overhead, and he who came as a dragon ends as an eagle, the bird of Jove, dealing down thunderbolts from a clear sky. I am pretty sure Milton had the contrast strongly in his mind of the Philistines at one moment gazing at the terrible Samson on the ground before them from their rows of seats, and not sure but he might rush or spring among them furiously, and the next moment experiencing destruction coming from him in the direction where all had seemed safe—i.e. vertically downwards. To bring out the contrast he resorts to the bold change of metaphor.' The abrupt transition here, and also to the next passage about the Phoenix, goes with the excitement of the speakers.

1699. *that self-begotten bird.* The Phoenix was supposed to be a unique and beautiful bird living in Arabia. It was believed that, after living for five centuries, it consumed itself in fire, and then rose again to life from its ashes. See *P.L.* v. 272.

1700. ARABIAN *woods.* Milton's conception varies the usual tradition, which represents the Phoenix as nesting in one solitary tree. Cf. *The Tempest*, III. iii. 21–24.

> Now I will believe
> That there are unicorns; that in Arabia
> There is one tree, the phoenix' throne; one phoenix
> At this hour reigning there.

Milton may well have remembered 'the sole Arabian tree' of Shakespeare's *The Phoenix and Turtle*.

1701. *That no second knows.* Only one phoenix is alive at any one time.

1707. The omission of many grammatical links in these last lines is in keeping with the triumphant rapidity of the chorus.

1709. *quit himself.* See 897 n. But there is also present here the idea that Samson has quitted his life.

1713. *Sons of* CAPHTOR. 'Caphtor' has been very variously identified, sometimes as Crete, sometimes as the Nile delta, and sometimes
as different parts of Asia Minor. The Old Testament generally
assumes that the Philistines were interlopers in Palestine. See
Jeremiah xlvii. 4 and Deuteronomy ii. 23.

1727. *lavers*. Cf. *Comus*, 838:

> And gave her to his daughters to imbathe
> In nectar'd lavers strew'd with Asphodil.

1732. *train*. 'Then his brethren and all the house of his father came
down, and took him, and brought *him* up, and buried him between
Zorah and Eshtaol in the buryingplace of Manoah his father'
(Judges xvi. 31).

1735. *Palm*: an emblem of victory. Christian martyrs were represented as holding palm branches to signify their triumph in death.

1748. *And ever best found in the close*. Merritt Hughes refers to the
closing choruses of Euripides' *Alcestis*, *Andromache*, *Bacchae*, and
Helen, all of which agree in the conclusion, that men cannot forecast
what the gods will do.

1749. *hide his face*. Cf. Psalm xxvii. 9: 'Hide not thy face far from
me; put not thy servant away in anger.'

1753. *band them*. See *P.L.* v. 714.

APPENDIX A

On the Verse

THE following notes are not meant to indicate any theory of metrical analysis; they have the practical purpose of indicating how the verse should be read.

The verse in the play is of two kinds; blank verse for dialogues, and partly rhymed lyric verse for the choruses and for certain monologues (ll. 80–109 and ll. 606–51).

(*a*) *The blank verse.* Milton's lines can conveniently be approached as if they were variations on a supposed 'normal' line of ten syllables with five stresses in rising rhythm. This pattern may be read into most of them without difficulty, as in:

> A líttle ónward lénd thy guíding hánd
> To thése dark stéps, a líttle fúrther ón;   (ll. 1–2)
>
> My ráce of glóry rún, and ráce of sháme,
> And Í shall shórtly bé with thém that rést.
>
> (ll. 597–8)

Even when a line departs widely from the supposed norm, the latter is in some way present to our mind, so that much of the effect of the poetry depends on the constant interplay between the supposed basic pattern and the varied rhythms we read.

Variations are obtained (i) by increasing the number of syllables, within certain limits; and (ii) by shifting the stresses, also within limits which can be defined.

(i) Milton increases the syllables in his lines mostly by means of so-called 'elisions'. He bases these on his personal

sense of what English words or sounds can be harmoniously
'run together', writing, for example:

> By wórse than hóstile deéds, *violáting the énds*   (l. 893)
>
> Retíring fróm the pópular noíse, I seék   (l. 16)
>
> Stálking with léss uncónsci'náble strídes.   (l. 1245)

These elisions are sometimes indicated by the spelling, as in
the last example, and 'Off'ring' (l. 26), 'Heav'n' (l. 1212),
'crestfall'n' (l. 1244). But even where a vowel is thus
omitted in the spelling, it is not to be omitted entirely in
speaking the verse: the pronunciation of elided syllables
is to be swifter, perhaps even a little slurred, but we are to
retain the sense of fullness and additional weight in the line.

    In the above examples of elision it will be seen that the
syllables run together are vowels, or vowels combined with
the liquid consonants *l*, *n*, *r*. But Milton in *Samson Agonistes*
goes beyond these limits in such lines as:

> The rést was mágnanímity tó remít   (l. 1470)
>
> And hé in thát calámitous príson léft.   (l. 1480)

Such lines are more frequent in this poem than in *Paradise
Lost* or *Paradise Regain'd*. Milton intends to give an effect
of dramatic speech, by means of these lighter rhythms.
This appears also in the greater frequency of lines with
so-called 'feminine endings', i.e. lines in which there are one
or more unstressed syllables after the tenth. The following
are examples:

> Sóme way or óther yet fúrther tó afflíct thee   (l. 1252)
>
> *Sámson*, of áll thy súfferings thínk the héaviest, (l. 445)
>
> Besídes, how víle, contémptiblé, ridículous   (l. 1361)
>
> Whó this high gíft of stréngth commítted tó me,
> In whát part lódged, how eásily beréft me,

> Únder the Séal of sílence cóuld not kéep,
> But wéakly tó a wóman múst revéal it
> O'ercóme with ímportúnity and téars.   (ll. 47–51)

(ii) The variety of stress is more difficult to illustrate, if only because there are never in fact five equal stresses in any line. Degrees of stress are practically impossible to define, but some will always be weaker than others. Milton's object is, as always, to obtain the greatest possible variety without destroying the effect of metrical unity. Almost all the supposed five stresses of the ten-syllable line can be shifted, but Milton observes two limitations. (i) He keeps a stress on the tenth syllable, which is the pivot of the line; and (ii) he makes one other stress fall on *either* the fourth *or* the sixth syllable. The first limitation appears everywhere, and needs no illustration. The second is seen in such lines as these:

> Th' unwórthier théy; whénce to this dáy they sérve
>
>   (l. 1216)
>
> Fór his péople of óld; what hínders nów?   (l. 1533)
>
> Thát invíncible *Sámson*, fár renówn'd.   (l. 341)

(*b*) *The choral verse.* Fundamentally the effect of the choruses depends on the combination of longer and shorter lines.[1] It follows that no one length of line is used consecutively often enough to impose itself as the expected length: there is a deliberate 'unexpectedness', a technique of 'surprise', in the differing line-lengths.

Milton sets himself upper and lower limits to the lengths

[1] This principle of lyric verse goes back to Greek and Latin poetry, appearing, for example, in Horace's Odes and Epodes. It is also the basis of Italian *canzone* form, and the tradition of the Italian *canzone* has contributed something essential to Milton's choruses (see F. T. Prince, *The Italian Element in Milton's Verse* (Oxford, 1954), chap. 9).

of his lines. The upper limit is a line of twelve syllables, the Alexandrine:

No strength of man, or fiercest wild beast could withstand;

(l. 137)

The lower limit is a line of four syllables.

O'er worn and soil'd.   (l. 123)

Between these extremes he uses lines of ten, eight, seven, six, and five syllables, varying them further by means of elisions and 'feminine endings'. Examples are:

Ten syllables:

O change beyond report, thought, or belief!   (l. 117)

Eight syllables:

But safest he who stood aloof,   (l. 135)

Seven syllables:

That heroic, that Renown'd,   (l. 125)

Six syllables:

With languish't head unpropt,   (l. 119)

Five syllables:

In the camp of *Dan*   (l. 1436)

As in the blank verse, laws of stress are needed to give an inner structure to these lines of different lengths, which are not simply groups of varying numbers of syllables. It is more difficult to describe how the stresses operate here, since Milton deliberately seeks to vary his rhythms as widely as possible. The basis is, however, the final stress in each line, as in the blank verse; but here this final stress becomes even more important, because the whole effect of the choruses depends on the differing line-lengths, and the end of each line has therefore to be marked distinctly.

The weight given to this last stress, whether it falls on the last syllable, the penultimate, or even the antepenultimate syllable (as in ll. 654–5), explains why Milton's lines even when unrhymed have something of the effect of rhyme. Assonance is frequent (see, for example, ll. 307–14 and ll. 629–31), and when full rhyme appears it grows naturally out of the form of verse, and is not merely 'tagged' to it.[1]

Rhyme contributes to various effects. It may be used for sonorous emphasis, especially in concluding lines, as in:

> Without reprieve adjudged to death,
> For want of well pronouncing *Shibboleth*.   (ll. 288–9)

It may increase the lyrical impetus of a whole series of comments, as in the chorus beginning:

> It is not virtue, wisdom, valour, wit,
> Strength, comeliness of shape, or amplest merit
> That woman's love can win or long inherit.
>   (ll. 1010 et seqq.)

The semi-choruses after Samson's death are quickened by more frequent rhyme as they sweep to a close (ll. 1687–1707); and the final chorus, as most conclusive and memorable, is rhymed throughout (ll. 1745–58).

These and other effects of the verse—particularly the pulsating rhythms which vary widely from one passage to another—can only be felt after repeated readings. In order to set off in the right direction the reader must give careful attention to line-endings; this should attune his ear to the harmonies of this kind of verse. The sense usually overflows the line, as in Milton's blank verse; and this is a part of the poetic effect. But the sense can be followed together with an emphasis on the line-lengths; sense and verse work together in a free but disciplined harmony.

[1] It is in Milton's use of rhyme that we find the most obvious resemblance to certain forms of Italian verse in the sixteenth century. See Prince, op. cit., chaps. 5 and 9.

On the Style

THE style of *Samson Agonistes* has sometimes been thought to show that Milton's powers were declining. Such a judgement is superficial. Milton deliberately modified the style of *Paradise Lost* when he wrote *Paradise Regain'd*, a poem on quite a different scale; and *Samson* required yet another variation of his manner. There is little or no room in drama for the rich descriptions and slow-moving sonorities of epic. This greater compression and severity is obvious in the dialogue; but the choruses too, though elaborate, are moulded by their place in the drama.

In the dialogue the barer style has nevertheless a wide range. The great statements are made with the utmost simplicity, as Samson's:

> Ask for this great Deliverer now, and find him
> Eyeless in *Gaza* at the Mill with slaves,   (ll. 40–41)

or:

> My race of glory run, and race of shame,
> And I shall shortly be with them that rest,   (ll. 597–8)

or Manoa's words of restraint to the Chorus:

> Nothing is here for tears, nothing to wail
> Or knock the breast, no weakness, no contempt,
> Dispraise or blame, nothing but well and fair,
> And what may quiet us in a death so noble.
>
>   (ll. 1721–4)

This flatness or bareness is indeed the prevailing style in the dialogue, and it shows that Milton appreciated a similar quality in the Greek dramatists. But one must not forget that all great drama uses a similar directness of expression for the most part; the effect of drama does not depend on continuously striking speech, but on the place of what is said in the whole situation, as in the intrinsically bald couplet spoken by Kent at the end of *King Lear*:

> I have a journey, sir, shortly to go;
> My master calls me, I must not say no.

But much of the dialogue is involved and disputatious; many speeches, and sometimes whole episodes, are taken up with justifying or rebutting some opinion or action (ll. 219–36; ll. 241–76; ll. 501–40 and 558–89; ll. 732–996; ll. 1178–1219; ll. 1319–42 and 1354–79). Milton's style is well adapted to this kind of highly emotional argumentation. He uses many of the methods and tricks of Latin oratory; and the Latinate vocabulary and syntax suggest cogent reasoning and fine distinctions. But in addition to this powerful, omnipresent, Latin element, Milton's style has much of the freedom and energy of expression that we find in the Elizabethans, and that makes possible Shakespeare's dramatic idiom. Like Shakespeare, Milton compresses, disregards grammar, and invents new idioms in a way which was to become impossible in literary English in the fifty years or so that followed his death. He takes advantage both of the Latin associations and of this almost Elizabethan exuberance to give his language a continuously unusual, arresting quality (see l. 424 n.). Above all, Milton makes his characters speak with a certain abruptness and incoherence which is very lifelike, despite the artifice of the language and the uniformity of the verse: the thought or emotion dictates the development of the sentences, often breaking through strict grammar and logic (see, for example, the changes of construction and abrupt transitions

of thought in ll. 1132–5, ll. 1338–41, and ll. 1495–1501).
In short, Milton has the dramatist's gift (which is perhaps
in essence only the poetic gift itself) of being able to convey
the mood or emotion of a character by the movement of
a speech. Dalila's coaxing, wavering cunning finds its
equivalent in the involved faltering sentences of her first
lines to Samson (ll. 732–47). Samson's indignant contempt
for Harapha pulses through his headlong retort and challenge to the giant's insults (ll. 1108–29).

The choruses are no less dramatic, and not only because
Milton has followed Aristotle's precept: 'The Chorus must
be regarded as one of the actors, and a part of the whole,
and as joining in the action.'[1] Milton's Chorus contributes
to the dramatic effect merely by its continuous presence:
it is able both to sympathize with Samson, and to give an
external point of view which makes his situation seem
simpler and more vivid. The style and movement of the
choruses vary according to the mood of the hero, the
Chorus taking its theme from him, descanting upon his
circumstances, thoughts, and emotions. In a slightly different
way the choruses achieve the same combination of complex
thought and passionate impulse that is found in the dialogue; here it is heightened by the form of the verse, verse
which is at once weighty and almost wantonly free, capable
of giving the impression of powerful feelings surging under
the control of grave thought.

The more closely we look at *Samson*, the more clearly
we can see it as a wonderful dramatic machine, in which
every part contributes to the whole, and no part can be
judged properly in isolation. The peculiarities of style of
both dialogue and choruses can only be understood in
relation to the total balance achieved at the end of the play.

[1] *Poetics* 18.

The Chronology of Milton's Life

1608 Born in Bread Street, Cheapside, London, 9 December. 'His father John Milton, an honest, worthy, and substantial citizen of London, by profession a scrivener' (Edward Phillips).

1620 Entered St. Paul's School.

1625 Matriculated at Christ's College, Cambridge, 9 April.
Charles I became King, March.

1629 Took B.A. degree, March.
Wrote *On the Morning of Christ's Nativity*, December.

1632 Took M.A. degree, July.
Settled at Horton in Buckinghamshire, where he lived until April 1638.

1633 William Laud became Archbishop of Canterbury.

1634 *Comus* performed at Ludlow Castle, 29 September.

1637 *Lycidas*, November.

1638–9 Left for continental tour in April 1638. Visited Paris, Florence, Rome, Naples, Venice, Geneva. Returned to England in August 1639.

1639 War with Scotland (First Bishops' War), March.

1639–40 Settled in London.

1640 Took as pupils his nephews, John and Edward Phillips.
Short Parliament. Second Bishops' War, August.
Long Parliament met, November. Laud and Strafford impeached.

1641–2 Begins pamphleteering for the abolition of episcopacy. Five tracts on this question: *Of Reformation in England*; *Of Prelatical Episcopacy*; *Animadversions upon the Remonstrant's Defence*; *The Reason of Church Government*; *Apology for Smectymnuus*.

1641 Execution of Strafford. Irish Rebellion.

1642 Married Mary Powell in May or June. She was the daughter of Richard Powell of Forest Hill, near Shotover, in Oxfordshire; and returned to her family, who were Royalists, after about a month of married life in London.
Preparations for civil war. The Battle of Edgehill, 23 October.

1643–5 Published the divorce tracts: *The Doctrine and Discipline of Divorce*; *The Judgement of Martin Bucer Concerning Divorce*; *Tetrachordon*; *Colasterion*.

1644 Prose tracts; *Of Education* and *Areopagitica*.
        Battles of Marston Moor and Newbury.

1645 Reconciliation with his wife, July or August.
        Moved to a house in Barbican.
        Victory of Cromwell's New Model army at the Battle of Naseby, June.

1645–6 *Miscellaneous Poems* published.

1646 First child, Anne, born 29 July.
        Powell family took refuge with the Miltons for a time.

1647 Milton's father died, March.

1648 Second child, Mary, born 25 October.

1649 Execution of Charles I, January.
        Milton wrote *The Tenure of Kings and Magistrates*, February.
        Was appointed Secretary for Foreign Tongues to the Council of State in March. Published *Eikonoklastes* October.

1651 Third child, John, born 16 March, died in infancy.
        Defensio pro Populo Anglicano, February.
        Granted assistance in office, owing to failing sight.

1652 Total blindness.
        Fourth child, Deborah, born 2 May. Mary Powell died, 5 May.

1653 Cromwell becomes Lord Protector.

1654 *Defensio Secunda*.

1655 *Defensio pro Se*.

1656 Married Katherine Woodcock, November.

1657 Daughter born, October.

1658 Wife and infant daughter died, February and March.
        Death of Cromwell, September.

1658 Two tracts arguing for religious freedom and against church establishment, February and August.
        Abdication of Richard Cromwell, May.

1660 *The Ready and Easy Way to Establish a Free Commonwealth*, March.
        Dismissed from office. Went into hiding in a friend's house in Bartholomew Close.
        The Restoration of Charles II, May. Act of Oblivion. Milton was exempted from prosecution through the influence of his friend Andrew Marvell and other Members of Parliament.

1663 Married Elizabeth Minshull, February.

     Moved to a house in Artillery Walk, Bunhill Fields.

1667 *Paradise Lost* published.

1671 *Paradise Regain'd* and *Samson Agonistes* published.

1673 Second and enlarged edition of *Miscellaneous Poems.*

     Published his last prose tract, a plea for mutual tolerance among
          Protestants: *Of True Religion, Heresy, Schism, Toleration; and
          What Best Means may be used against the Growth of Popery.*

1674 Second edition of *Paradise Lost.*

     Milton died, 8 November; buried in St. Giles', Cripplegate.